The

CURIOUS

KITCHEN

GARDENER

Frontispiece: Long bean plant
Copyright © 2025 by Linda Ziedrich. All rights reserved.

All photographs are by the author.
Icon art by The Noun Project: Adriansyah (pancake), Arkinasi (lemonade), Courtney Baker (romaine lettuce), dDara (poppy), Deemak Daksina (jar), Edwin PM (sorrel), Edy Subiyanto (mint), Eskak (tomato), Giangiacomo Galliani (wok), IYIKON (quince), Juraj Sedlák (grape leaf), Kmg Design (parsnip, soy beans, strawberry), N.Style (leaf grape), Olena Panasovska (string beans), P Thanga Vignesh (corn), Pronto Illustration (lettuce), Rahmat (soup), sentya Irma (lavender), Singlar (melon), Smashing Stocks (walnut), Soetarman Atmodjo (cup), Savannah Vize (fennel), Teewara soontorn (potato slices)

Timber Press
Workman Publishing
Hachette Book Group, Inc.
1290 Avenue of the Americas
New York, New York 10104
timberpress.com

Timber Press is an imprint of Workman Publishing, a division of Hachette Book Group, Inc. The Timber Press name and logo are registered trademarks of Hachette Book Group, Inc.
Printed in China on responsibly sourced paper
Cover and text design by Vincent James
The publisher is not responsible for websites (or their content) that are not owned by the publisher.
The Hachette Speakers Bureau provides a wide range of authors for speaking events. To find out more, go to hachettespeakersbureau.com or email hachettespeakers@hbgusa.com.

ISBN 978-1-64326-231-4
A catalog record for this book is available from the Library of Congress.

The

CURIOUS
KITCHEN
GARDENER

Uncommon Plants
& How to Eat Them

Linda Ziedrich

Timber Press
Portland, Oregon

To my blog readers,
with thanks for all
you've taught me

CONTENTS

Preface | 9

Introduction | 13

Preface

This book reflects forty-five years of gardening experience and experimentation. My life as a gardener began in Palo Alto, California, where, in the backyard of a rental house, my then brand-new husband, Robert, and I sowed seeds of many kinds of vegetables and ended up with nothing but mustard.

During six subsequent years in Somerville, Massachusetts, I tended a community garden plot, took a Master Gardener course, and, for two seasons, ran the city's community garden program. For another six years, in Ben Lomond, California, I kept a big vegetable garden and cared for an assortment of fruit trees as well.

This helped prepare me for life on a small farm in Oregon's Willamette Valley—a few miles west of West Scio—where my serious horticultural work began. I set about restoring depleted, compacted soil for a vegetable garden, and Robert and I replanted the orchard, which had been cut to the ground. He built a greenhouse for raising vegetable starts. With three growing children to feed, I set out about one hundred tomato plants each year and half as many pepper plants. And I planted more and more unusual food plants, both fruits and vegetables, and both annuals and perennials. Using produce from the Ben Lomond and Scio gardens I wrote three cookbooks, *Cold Soups*, *The Joy of Pickling*, and *The Joy of Jams, Jellies, and Other Sweet Preserves*. The last especially emphasized uncommon fruits, such as quinces, red and black currants, elderberries, and even black nightshade.

In 2015, with the children grown and gone, Robert and I returned to city life. Near downtown Lebanon, Oregon, we bought a little Craftsman house on a quarter-acre lot. Robert built a greenhouse, again, and he made raised beds for vegetables. I planted fruit trees in the front yard. The experiments continued, though now I needed to choose varieties more carefully and to sow crops consecutively, never leaving ground bare. Eventually I expanded into the city's first municipal community garden, where the all-day sun allows corn and melons to thrive.

Although this book is part cookbook, it focuses more on the garden than the kitchen. The plants included are little known or underappreciated. Their edible parts are seldom available in grocery stores. But these plants tend to be particularly useful for home gardeners, over large temperate regions. The plants I've chosen have interesting pasts, too. You can't really know a garden plant without growing it, but each chapter should give you a thorough introduction to the plant's history, growing and harvest requirements, and uses. I hope that this book will inspire you to try growing some of these plants and that at least a few will become essential to your life as a gardener and as a cook.

The thirty-three chapters are arranged chronologically, according to time of harvest, from early spring through winter. Each includes a recipe to get you started incorporating the plant in your family's diet.

Introduction

Americans are often at a loss to describe their national cuisine. Hotdogs, hamburgers, pizza, spaghetti? Those foods are now beloved around the world. Pizza is seldom made at home, and hotdogs are never made from scratch. Even burgers are usually eaten out. What foods are really ours? Which do we prepare at home, besides spaghetti?

The foods we grow ourselves, in our backyards, front yards, and community gardens, are often overlooked. The U.S. Department of Agriculture explicitly omits from its agricultural statistics foods grown for consumption on the homestead rather than for sale. The bounty of our gardens is excluded from the gross national product. The sharing of homegrown foods among neighbors and friends is seldom reported to the Internal Revenue Service, because money is rarely exchanged. Kitchen gardening is all but invisible to economists and most government officials.

The kitchen gardener feels unseen, unknown. Media discussions about food often seem odd and alienating. With access to edible commodities from every hemisphere, professional chefs create jarring combinations of foods of different seasons. Cookbook authors expect us to make a long shopping list before we can follow a recipe. Nutritionists generalize about "the modern Western diet" and food products' constituents and values, as if a giant 'Granny Smith' apple grown in an industrial orchard is equivalent to your little, unsprayed 'Ashmead's Kernel'. A hunger for authenticity has led to a popular infatuation with foreign foods, foods from places where cooks and eaters still feel connected to the land. Yet few Americans seem to understand what it means to create wholesome meals, day after day, from what is on hand in the garden, the cellar, the freezer, and the fridge, without continual recipe searches and runs to the supermarket.

Why do those of us who grow what we eat choose to live this way? Keeping a kitchen garden, preserving its bounty, and making meals from scratch takes substantial time, and combining what's on hand in appealing ways, day after day, requires a lot of creativity. But those of us who don't mind a little dirt under the fingernails have plenty of reasons to center our lives on homegrown food. Like all gardeners, we love fresh air and sunshine. We also like limiting trips to the supermarket. We like saving money, and we can save a lot if we use homemade compost as fertilizer, store seeds from year to year, and swap them among our friends (our bank accounts would be bigger, certainly, if we gave up the hours in the garden and kitchen for more hours at a desk job or other paid employment, but that would be an act of desperation). We like knowing that our produce is clean, free of pesticides and other contaminants, and we prefer the taste of just-picked fruits and vegetables over produce that has been sitting in warehouses and on trucks for days or weeks. We may enjoy eating parts of plants missing from supermarket produce, such as beet greens, garlic scapes, and broccoli stems. We savor the intense flavors of foods from plants that haven't been overwatered and overfertilized, as those grown on gigantic farms usually have been. We may be eager to lessen our dependence on the industrial food system, with all the harm that it does animals and workers. Most of all, perhaps, we like witnessing the natural cycles of energy from soil to seed to flower to fruit to compost. We like feeling that we ourselves are part of nature's cycles.

The kitchen gardener's life isn't romantic or exotic, but it is rich. For people like us, culture begins in the soil. What seeds you sow and what plants you cultivate determines what you cook and what you feed those who gather around your table. As your family braids garlic, presses apples, roasts chiles, and winnows seeds together, year after year, you are developing a way of life. Even if you spend much of your time in an office and send the children off to school every day, your family has its own foodways, which determine what you pack in the lunch bags, what you offer visitors and share with the neighbors, what your children might like to eat when they're older, and what they might feed their own children and friends. Yours is not the "modern Western diet."

You have your unique diet, and your unique way of life, and they are part of an ever-changing web of local and regional foodways that responds subtly as you interact with other gardeners, cooks, and eaters.

Your own foodways aren't immutable. They evolve quickly if you like novelty and have easy access to new plant materials and growing information. An increasing number of small seed and nursery companies bring us the latest breeders' innovations. Researchers at land-grant universities develop cultivars that thrive in their states. Seed Savers Exchange, a nearly half-century-old seed bank and seed-sharing network, teaches us about almost-forgotten garden heirlooms, and companies like Seeds from Italy and Kitazawa Seed Company sell us what's popular in other parts of the world. Sometimes you try a strange vegetable or a new variety that you'll never want to plant again. But, if you take the best of what these sources have to offer, your garden gets more productive each year. You choose your processing methods and develop your cooking style to accommodate the abundance.

When I first started gardening in Oregon's Willamette Valley, most of the vegetable gardens I saw included only sweet corn, snap beans, and tomatoes. More adventurous gardeners added head cabbage and bulb onions, both bought as nursery starts. These gardeners were limiting their work to the warmest, driest months of the year and harvesting, often in great quantities, the foods they valued most. That made sense. But I had to wonder if this kind of gardening wasn't a little boring—and if the meals prepared from the produce weren't boring, too.

This book is for more curious kitchen gardeners. It is curiosity that makes us want to try every new species or cultivar that might perform well in our soil and climate. From these trials we end up reserving space each year for lesser-known plants that have become dear to us. We may stop growing head cabbage and bulb onions, which can be bought cheaply year-round and which keep best in industrial storage conditions. We may focus instead on foods that are expensive to buy but easy to grow at home, such as artichokes and asparagus. Each time we make a shift in the garden from cabbage to artichokes, from onions to asparagus, from the common to the uncommon, we are shifting our household's diet as well. We are signing up for adventures in the garden, in the kitchen, and at the table.

Asparagus and artichokes are perennials; you don't till up their beds every fall. When we add edible perennials to our gardens, we get more variety for less effort. We may want to include rhubarb and Jerusalem artichoke, chives and other perennial alliums, and all kinds of perennial herbs. As we try to find places for all of these, the kitchen garden may end up intruding into our ornamental beds. And why not? The edibles may look lovely scattered among the plants we have planted for their looks and fragrance.

We may even find ourselves eating our ornamentals. Violet and calendula and nasturtium flowers are tasty, and very pretty in salads. Nasturtium leaves are miniature edible plates, and nasturtium seeds, pickled, taste like capers. The buds of old-fashioned daylilies are excellent fried (beware of the hybrids, which can be toxic); the seeds of opium poppy are tasty and nutritious; and lavender provides an intriguing flavor in many foods. Roses are heavenly in preserves and syrups; and rose hips make a delectable and nutritious butter. Sour and tannic little fruits on our trees and shrubs—Oregon grape, hawthorn, mountain ash—often make excellent jellies.

When we look at our garden in a fresh way, as an integrated whole, as our year-round habitat, we may also begin eating the weeds. Dandelions truly are refreshing in spring, miner's lettuce is a delight, and that clump of mushrooms, if you can identify them with certainty, may become an annual succulent treat. We may find ourselves letting the purslane and pokeweed grow just because we like to eat them now and then.

Because we aren't just summer gardeners, our family's diet better reflects the seasons. Each season seems hallowed by the special foods we eat in it. If there is little food fresh from the garden in winter, there are foods we have pickled or canned or frozen in the fall and put away just for this lean time. My blog, *A Gardener's Table*, is a record of one gardener's long years of experimentation and refinement, in the garden and in the kitchen. Through this work, and through my family's changing tastes and dietary needs, has evolved our own cuisine, at once American and unique. Your family's cuisine is different; it reflects *your* tastes, *your* needs. Most of all, it reflects your soil and climate, which determine what you can grow well. My stories may inspire you to repeat some of my experiments, to try something I haven't thought of, or just to take more pride in your own kitchen garden and the life you have built around it. If nothing more, I hope you'll enjoy this taste of life in my garden and kitchen.

Sweet Violets

As everybody knows, violets are blue—except when they are pink, or white, or mauve, or white tinged with lavender. This is what I learned after moving to Lebanon, Oregon, and tilling the 7 ft. (2 m) wide planting strip stretching the breadth of our lot between the sidewalk and the curb.

Because we had a corner lot, long planting strips surrounded the house on two sides. I started with the one in front. It held two young shade trees and nothing else but Bermuda grass and moss. To kill the Bermuda grass, I dug it all out and then covered the entire strip with plastic sheeting. Several months later, I removed the plastic, planted the strip with shrubs and other perennials, and spread several inches of bark mulch among them.

I don't know how many decades the seeds of *Viola odorata* had lain dormant under the grass and moss, but now they sprouted, right through several inches of bark mulch. Soon mounds of dark green, heart-shaped leaves formed a groundcover around the shrubs and other perennials.

The following spring the violets began blooming. Now I had only to open the front door to fill my head with their unique sweet scent. (Easterners: Don't confuse your native *Viola cucullata* or *V. sororia* with *V. odorata*. Your nose should tell the difference.)

But few of the violet plants produced blue flowers. Shades of pink predominated in the planting strip, and where I'd torn up parts of the shaded, mossy back lawn I found white violets and some that were mixed blue and white.

In Europe and Asia, the homeland of the sweet violet, odd colors apparently arose spontaneously. Beginning in the nineteenth century, breeders named and propagated selections they particularly liked. The seeds must have sold widely. I imagine a long-ago resident of my house tearing open a packet of mixed-color violet seeds, sprinkling them up and down the planting strip, and tossing the leftovers into the backyard. The plants would have spread by seed and by runners until someone tore them up and planted lawn in their place.

If you don't have violets growing as weeds in your garden, you can plant them. Violet seeds should be sown in fall and thinly covered with soil. You can start them in a flat, if you like, and leave the flat in the shade over the winter. If you've missed the opportunity for fall planting, you can stratify the seeds to help them break their dormancy and begin germinating. Instructions for stratifying vary. Most people mix the seeds with a little moist sand in a freezer bag and keep the bag in a refrigerator for four to six weeks.

A few seedhouses sell seeds of old violet cultivars, mostly from the nineteenth century: 'Reine de Neiges' (white, from Swallowtail Garden Seeds), 'Queen Charlotte' (violet, from Select Seeds and Hazzard's Seeds), 'Rosina' (pink, from Select), and 'Czar' (blue, from Swallowtail). At least one nursery, Valleybrook Gardens of British Columbia, is still breeding violets; Valleybrook sells its 'Classy Pink', 'Intense Blue', and 'Bridewhite' violets as potted plants to garden centers in Canada and along both U.S. coasts.

Maybe you wonder who would pay for a potted weed. Violets, after all, can be invasive. But even today some people take their violets so seriously that they join the American Violet Society to study, celebrate, and promote the little plants.

I suspect that these violet aficionados fuss mainly over the appearance of the blossoms. I focus instead on the plant's uses. Violets are not only among the earliest garden flowers to bloom, and they are not only fragrant. Since they don't much object to mowing, they are also an attractive addition to a shady lawn. The fresh blossoms are lovely in a salad, and they can be crystallized—by dipping them in beaten egg white and then in sugar—for decorating desserts (if you're worried about salmonella, use a pasteurized egg). The dried blossoms and leaves, in a tisane, are said to soothe headaches and relieve insomnia. Violet liqueur is essential for cocktails such as the Aviator, and violet syrup can be a pleasant coloring and flavoring for white or sparkling wine, meringues, and ices. You might even make violet ice cubes: Lay violets in an

ice-cube tray, fill the tray half-full of water, freeze the tray, and then top with water and freeze the tray again.

A modern use for violets—because it requires packaged pectin, a twentieth-century innovation—is violet jelly. High-methoxyl pectin, the regular kind, requires both sugar and acid for gelling (low-methoxyl pectin requires no acid or sugar for gelling, but in my experience this pectin produces cloudy jelly—and keep in mind that if your jelly is low in both sugar and acid you should not can it). The acid I add comes from lemon juice, which also enhances the flavor of the jelly, and it has another effect, one that might impress your children: A little lemon transforms violet "juice" from the deep blue of blue violets to a pinker shade, nearly as pink as some of my pink violets. Much of the violet aroma is sadly lost in cooking, but if you start out with plenty of blossoms you will produce a jelly that is intensely flavorful as well as gorgeous.

In recent years my violet groundcover has declined. As the climate has warmed, the blossoms either haven't appeared at all or have been immediately scorched. But the seeds are so many and so persistent that I know, one cool spring, I will again be able to make violet jelly.

Violet Jelly

MAKES 1 ¼ PINTS (600 ML)

When you pick your violets, you needn't remove the green calyx at the base of each flower. Even a bit of stem here and there won't hurt your jelly.

Although I used Ball's Classic pectin in this recipe, you should feel free to substitute another brand of high-methoxyl pectin; just know that you may need to adjust the method according to the manufacturer's instructions. Note that the violets require a long soaking time, and plan accordingly.

4 cups (1 L) blue sweet violets

2 cups (473 mL) water, boiled and then left to cool for about 2 minutes

3 tablespoons strained lemon juice

3 tablespoons Ball Classic pectin

1 ½ cups (300 g) sugar

1. Put the violets in a bowl and pour the water over them. Cover the bowl and let it sit at room temperature for 8 to 12 hours.

2. Strain the liquid through a jelly bag, squeezing the bag to extract the last of the blue liquid. (Don't worry, squeezing it won't make the juice cloudy.) Add a little water, if needed, to equal 2 cups (473 mL).

3. Stir the lemon juice into the violet liquid. The liquid will turn a pinker shade. Pour the liquid into a preserving pan. Gradually sprinkle over the pectin, and stir it in. Bring the mixture to a full boil, and immediately add the sugar. Bring the mixture back to a boil. Boil it for 1 minute.

4. Remove the pan from the heat. Ladle the syrup into sterilized ½ or ¼ pt. (235 or 118 mL) Mason jars. Add two-piece caps, and process the jars in a boiling-water or steam canner for 5 minutes.

Radical Ways *with* Radishes

The big difference between cooks who garden and those who don't is that the former start with what's available. Market shoppers may claim to do the same—to begin their meals by buying produce that's fresh and in season. But shoppers usually buy only what they can use right away, and so seldom must deal with excess. Every success in the garden brings with it a burden—heaps of vegetables or fruits that must be dried, pickled, canned, stored in the cellar, or crammed into the refrigerator. The last is easiest, when the harvest isn't *too* big, but before the veggies go sad and limp in the fridge the gardener had better wash the soil from her hands and start cooking. If she is short on ideas, it's time to consult the cookbooks.

That's what I did one day, after bringing in a pile of 'French Breakfast' radishes. Nearly everybody eats radishes raw—in salads if not at breakfast with butter. And, of course, radishes are good for fermenting and vinegar-pickling, in various ways. But surely they are most digestible cooked. If I wanted to put a lot of radishes into our stomachs right away, I needed to cook them.

I found inspiration in Irene Kuo's book *The Key to Chinese Cooking*. In it, Irene shares a recipe for a pork and radish soup. I had no raw pork on hand,

but I had the remains of a half brined ham. And I had a potential ingredient Irene may never have considered: a pot full of fragrant leek broth.

The leek broth resulted from an earlier harvest the same day. Needing to clear a bed so I could plant it with tomatoes, I had brought in an armload of leeks. Since I had plenty more leeks in another bed, these could all go into the freezer. I washed them, sliced them, and blanched them for a minute in batches before spreading them on cookie sheets, freezing them, and vacuum-packing them. Now the blanching liquid smelled too good to throw out.

So I made a radish soup like Irene's, but with a leek- and ham-flavored broth and bits of leftover ham. I served it over buckwheat noodles, with a bowl of raw arugula to tear and add at will. What a simple and satisfying meal!

When I told this story later, a friend gently chided me for throwing away the radish tops. Why hadn't I added them to the soup? Radish tops are generally too prickly to eat raw, but they are entirely edible when cooked, and just as tasty as most greens in the *Brassica* genus (which includes cabbage, kale, collard, mustard, and Asian greens such as bok choy). So the next time I made a radish soup I included the greens along with the roots.

If you let a radish begin to set seed, you can enjoy another underappreciated part of the plant: the green pods.

One radish variety that I've grown with great success is the Italian 'Candela di Fuoco', "Candle of Fire." It's a long, skinny radish—up to 10 in. (25 cm), with

carmine skin and a crisp white interior. 'Candela di Fuoco' is the only radish that I've been able to plant in fall and harvest in spring without its bolting prematurely.

To replenish my stock of 'Candela di Fuoco' radish seeds one year, I let a single plant go to seed. It grew into a lovely bush, about 3 ft. (1 m) tall and wide, with pink blooms that continued to appear as the seed pods matured and dried. Although I loved the look of the plant, it was taking up bed space that I needed for other things. As soon as I could collect a few handfuls of dried pods I uprooted the plant.

Most of the pods were still green and tender, but I couldn't let them go to waste. Although they were quite small, I collected enough to fill a pint jar. I added a garlic clove, a hot pepper, and a tarragon sprig, and then I heated a half-cup each of cider vinegar and water with a little salt. I poured the liquid over the pods to cover them, and voilà: a radish-pod pickle. I wasn't quite done, though. I left the jar out for eight hours or so, turning the tightly capped jar two or three times, and then I added a tablespoon of olive oil, refrigerated the jar, and waited at least a week before eating the tart, crisp little pickles.

Some radish varieties, called rat-tail, are grown specifically for their pods. Usually they are a few inches long, but some Asian varieties can grow up to 12 in. (30 cm) long. Most rat-tail radish pods are green; others are a stunning magenta. Rat-tail radishes typically have tender pods. With other radish varieties, you must harvest your pods carefully. Pick them when they are nearly fully developed but still quite green. You might taste one or two to be sure you can tell the tender from the tough.

Tender radish pods are as delicious stir-fried as pickled.

Ham *and* Radish Soup *with* Leek Broth

SERVES 4

Even though you're using radish leaves in this soup, you might accompany it with raw arugula, to add to the bowls at the table. With its distinct, meaty flavor, arugula is likely to be ready in your garden at the same time you're harvesting radishes.

8 cups (1.9 L) leek broth, preferably unsalted, from blanching or cooking leeks

12 ounces (340 g) ham bone(s)

6 quarter-size slices ginger

12 ounces (340 g) radish roots

12 ounces (340 g) ham, diced small

Salt (optional)

Radish tops, cut into 2 in. (5 cm) lengths

Fresh or dried buckwheat or wheat noodles

---

1. Strain the broth, if needed, into a large saucepan. Add the bone(s) and ginger. Simmer the broth for about 1 ½ hours.

2. Cut the radishes into ½ by 1 in. (1.25 by 2.5 cm) pieces. Depending on the variety and size, you can slice the radishes into quarters or eighths, or you can roll-cut them, slicing diagonally with a quarter-turn between slices; this maximizes the cut surface area of each piece and promotes even cooking and flavor absorption.

3. Add the radishes and ham to the broth. Simmer the soup until the radishes are tender, about 30 minutes longer. Taste the broth and add salt, if needed; the ham will likely have provided enough. Add the radish tops and stir slowly. The soup is ready as soon as the radish tops have wilted.

4. Before the soup has finished simmering, cook the noodles in boiling water. Drain the noodles, rinse them in cold water, and divide them among large soup bowls. Ladle the hot soup over the noodles.

29

Angelica, *Bitter and* Sweet

Someone once asked why I first planted angelica. My response was the sheepish one common among gardeners: I saw the plant in a nursery. But, well, it was cheap! Just a 3 in. (7.5 cm) pot! And I thought angelica might grow well in the bed in the damp lawn south of our Scio house. Besides, I once had a German pen pal named Angelika.

Angelica is a member of the family Umbelliferae, or Apiaceae, which provides an assortment of flavors for the kitchen (other members include parsley, carrot, parsnip, fennel, anise, coriander, celery, dill, cumin, lovage, and caraway). Like many of its cousins, angelica is a biennial or short-lived perennial; the seeds sprout after they're dropped in the summer, and then the little plants overwinter before sending up tall seed stalks the following summer or, especially in colder places, in the third or fourth year. *Angelica archangelica*, the garden variety, can grow as tall as 8 ft. (2.5 m). Tasting the bitter leaves might make you avoid this plant as potentially poisonous, and in fact the herb has been used more as medicine than as food. The leaves, seeds, stems, and roots of angelica species have all served as remedies for various complaints, especially bronchial and digestive problems (the stems are "grateful to a feeble stomach," wrote Maud Grieve in *A Modern Herbal*). But in the kitchen angelica has many uses. The dried leaves have been used as tea and as a bittering agent in beer. The roots and seeds have flavored wine and liqueurs and gin, the ground dried root has been added to baked goods, and the fresh leaves have flavored salads, soups, stews, custards, ice cream, and other desserts.

A few years after I planted my little *Angelica archangelica* start, I had let angelica plants entirely take over the bed in the damp lawn. So I was happy when I came upon a description of two European angelica species, *A. archangelica* and *A. sylvestris*, in Patience Gray's *Honey from a Weed*:

> Both these angelicas grow wild near abandoned ruins and damp places. In February the Salentines [the people of the Salerno, the heel of the Italian boot] go feverishly in search of them. This is the moment when the incipient flower-heads are still enclosed in their sheaths right up against the greenish-purple stem. You cut these sheaths with a knife.

So, angelica could serve as a vegetable!

I headed straight to the garden to cut some of the little sheaths. According to Patience, I could boil or grill them and serve them with olive oil and a little wine vinegar, or I could boil, flour, and fry them. The sheaths would taste strong and bitter, I knew, although Patience described them as "aromatic and faintly sweet." British by birth, she had adopted Italian tastes; she seemed to truly *like* bitter weeds. I might prefer the bitterness softened with grease and starch. So, I decided to fry my sheaths.

My angelica sheaths came in various sizes. I tore into some of the large ones because I could feel bits of hard stalk inside. Within each large sheath I found a smaller one, or, usually, two. Sometimes the larger of the two contained two more little sheaths. The soft green pouches within pouches reminded me of Matryoshka dolls, or the Cat in the Hat, with all the little and littler cats hidden beneath his topper.

A tender green flower head peeked out from one slightly open sheath, looking like a strangely delicate broccoli floret. Perhaps this sheath was past its prime? I decided to use it anyway.

To make *zavirne fritte* ("fried angelica," a specialty in southern Italy), you boil the sheaths "for a few minutes," instructed Patience. I hurried to put a pot of salted water on to boil, because the cut edges of the angelica had begun

browning immediately after harvest. I boiled the sheaths vigorously for five minutes. This was perhaps a bit too long; one or two began to fall apart, though the open sheath turned out fine.

I drained off the now vivid-green water, covered the sheaths with cold water, and let them sit in the water for an hour, as Patience instructed. The soaking, I supposed, would moderate their bitterness.

After an hour had passed, I drained the sheaths and dried them on a towel. I rolled them first in beaten egg and then in salted and peppered flour before frying them in hot oil until the coating turned golden.

We ate the fried sheaths immediately, while I finished cooking dinner. This was the right thing to do, because zavirne fritte are best hot; the warm, crisp coating counteracts the bitterness.

Angelica sheaths *are* bitter, more bitter than radicchio, I'd say, though less so than dandelions. The incipient flower heads inside are tender and sweetly perfumed in the odd, medicinal way of angelica—rather like horehound, licorice, or anise, but at the same time unique. My husband detects hints of roses and grass in the flavor, which he also finds soapy (soap makers take note: angelica might provide a wonderful new aroma for your products). Angelica's strong aroma often mystifies and even scares people unfamiliar with it, but I think it can grow on you. To know this flavor, you must try zavirne fritte, an angelica-flavored liqueur such as Chartreuse, or, perhaps best of all, candied angelica.

Although candying vegetables is an ancient craft, candied angelica stems were popular in England as late as the 1960s, especially for decorating the tops of cakes. You might cut a piece of candied stem into a diamond shape, say, and place it beside a glacéed cherry. You could also cut the stems into rounds and add the rounds to batter or sprinkle them over ice cream. You might even cut the stems into short pieces and dip them in chocolate. I think candied angelica is wonderful in biscotti, gingerbread, and fruitcake. In France, where candied angelica is still produced commercially, it is featured in a special (but simple) cake, *galette charentaise*.

Making angelica candy traditionally requires a visit to the angelica bed in April. Early May should be fine, too, provided the stems are still green, not purplish—although you shouldn't wait until the plant blooms, which according to European tradition happens on the 8th of May, the feast day of St. Michael the Archangel. Use only thick stems, and cut away the leaves and leaf stems.

I developed my candying method from several old, slow recipes. Here's what you do: Cook the stems in a pot of boiling water until they are tender (their sharp, bitter aroma will fill the air), or for four to six minutes. Drain them, rinse them in cold water, and then rub off the thin skins. Put the stems into a bowl, pour over a syrup made of equal parts sugar and water, and then weight the stems with a small plate. The next day, drain off the syrup, boil to thicken it a bit, and pour it over the angelica. Repeat this process the next day and the day after. On the following day, pour off the syrup again, boil it to the thread stage (215 to 235°F, or 102 to 112°C), add the angelica stems, and bring the syrup back to the thread stage. Drain the stems, and let them dry on a rack in a warm place. When they are dry, dust them with sugar and store them in an airtight container.

If you'd like a simpler way to use angelica stems, consider pairing them with rhubarb in preserves. Rhubarb-angelica preserves are a traditional Northern European treat. I've read that Icelanders use equal parts rhubarb and angelica in their preserves, but I suggest starting with 1 part angelica to 2 parts rhubarb. Gather the angelica stems when they are still green. For the prettiest color, use rhubarb that is green, not red.

Make your preserves this way. For about 1 lb. (454 g) rhubarb and ½ lb. (227 g) angelica, use ⅔ cup (158 mL) water and 2 cups (400 g) sugar. Slowly dissolve the sugar in the water in a preserving pan, and bring the syrup to a boil. While the syrup heats, cut the rhubarb into 1 in. (2.5 cm) pieces and the angelica stems into slender rings. Add the angelica and rhubarb to the hot syrup, and simmer the mixture very gently for an hour or longer, stirring very little if at all, until the rhubarb is quite tender and the syrup is somewhat thickened (if you prefer a jammy texture, stir all you like). Keep in mind that the preserves will thicken more as they cool.

In May, keep an eye on your angelica plants again, so you can enjoy their blooms and the multitude of insects they attract. On the farm, my angelica would bloom precisely on the 8th of May, and would immediately swarm with wasps of every imaginable kind.

The little yellowish angelica flowers are soon replaced with seeds (or, technically, fruits). They will drop to the ground as they dry, and in spring you will have many little plants. If you want to save seeds for planting elsewhere, collect them, let them dry thoroughly, and chill them for a few weeks before planting in early spring (don't expect them to keep for another year—they won't retain their viability for that long). To plant, sprinkle the seeds on the soil surface; they need light to germinate. You can transplant the babies when they are 3 to 4 in. (8 to 10 cm) tall. You can also divide older plants, in fall or early spring. Give your angelica plants plenty of water and mulch. If you live in a hot place, give them partial shade as well.

If you don't have angelica in your garden yet, it's easiest to get started with a nursery-grown plant. If you can't find one, or if your growing conditions seem unsuitable for *Angelica archangelica*, you may be tempted to collect seed in the wild. Angelica grows all over the Northern Hemisphere, in about ninety species that all look similar and are presumably edible (although one of them, in California, is known as poison angelica). The various species are, of course, adapted to their regions. Although I think of angelica as a wetland plant, some species thrive in hot, dry places, including Nevada. I long refrained from planting *A. archangelica* in my city garden because the soil is light and fast-draining, but last fall I collected seeds of *A. lucida* on the Oregon coast. I hesitated to gather the seeds at first, because angelica looks much like other wild plants in the same family, including poisonous water hemlock, *Cicuta*. But then I sniffed the plant. The angelica fragrance was unmistakable. One seed sprouted, and the sprout has grown into a handsome potted planted, with young leaves like shiny leather. You should be very careful, though, in harvesting any part of a wild angelica plant. If you are uncertain of the species, be sure you know at least that it truly is angelica and not water hemlock, which often grows alongside it.

You might grow angelica only for its beauty and the pollen that delights the wasps and flies in your garden. But eating angelica is a lovely thing to try, even if you do it just once. You will no doubt marvel at the taste, and, if you believe the old-time herbalists, you will leave the table fortified against witches, evil spirits, and the plague.

Zavirne Fritte

To keep the angelica sheaths from browning, you might put the pot of water on to boil even before you harvest. Angelica sheaths require an hour of rest in cold water after boiling, so plan accordingly.

Freshly gathered angelica sheaths

Vegetable oil, for frying

All-purpose flour, for dredging

Salt and freshly ground black pepper

1 or more eggs, beaten

1. Bring a large pot of salted water to a boil. Put the angelica sheaths in the pot, and boil for 3 to 4 minutes.

2. Drain the hot water, and cover the angelica sheaths with cold water. Let them rest in the water for an hour.

3. Drain off the water, lay the sheaths on a towel, and pat them dry.

4. Heat at least 3 in. (7.5 cm) of oil in a pot to 350°F (175°C). Put the flour into a wide bowl, and stir in salt and pepper to taste.

5. When the oil is hot, turn the angelica sheaths, one at a time, first in the beaten egg and then in the seasoned flour. Shake each one lightly before dropping it into the hot oil. Fry only a few at a time, turning them gently. Remove each sheath to paper towels or newspapers when its coating turns golden.

6. Serve the hot angelica sheaths immediately, alone as an appetizer or alongside meat or whatever else you're having for dinner. Or try them as dessert, with honey or powdered sugar or both.

Bamboo
for Dinner

Sometimes the best strategy for managing pests is to eat them. Cajuns savor stewed nutria. Mexicans crunch fried grass-hoppers. The French swallow butter-soaked snails. And I eat runaway bamboo.

After beautifully screening my bee and compost yard for fifteen years, my bamboo hedge got out of hand, pushing up shoots as far as 10 ft. (3 m) from its designated territory and right through the heavy-duty landscape fabric at the base of my raised beds. The shoots can grow as much as 12 in. (30 cm) in a day.

Why was I fool enough to plant running bamboo without walling it in? Actually, I had no regrets about this, most of the time. The 25 ft. (7.5 m) long hedge not only looked lovely year-round, but it also provided all the stakes and trellis material that my friends and I could use, and on summer afternoons it shaded one of my beds so I could grow lettuce there.

But I shouldn't have started using an overhead sprinkler. Out of laziness, I was watering not only the raised beds but the grass paths between and around them. In doing so I was watering the bamboo roots, and in response they were expanding into a bamboo forest. I had to get my bamboo under control. Digging a shallow trench around the hedge was one way; eating the shoots was another.

I don't know what species of bamboo I had; the nursery had sold it simply as "green bamboo." According to the American Bamboo Society website, there are about 1,450 species of bamboo, many of them native to Asia, but others

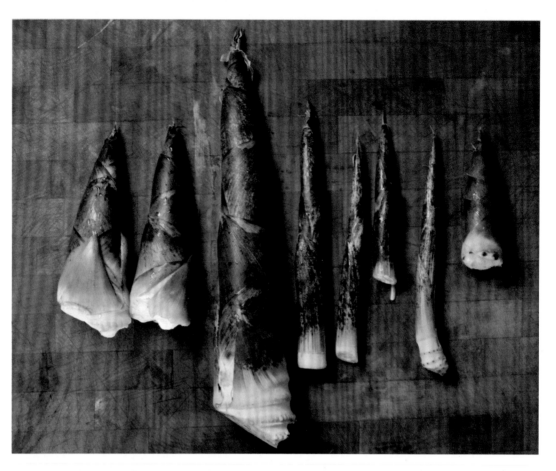

to Australia, Africa, or North or South America. Most, if not all, species have edible shoots. My bamboo grew about 15 ft. (4.6 m) high, and the canes were no more than about 1 in. (2.5 cm) in diameter.

Because bamboo species vary so much, it's hard to find reliable advice about harvesting and preparing the shoots. Some people say to cut them a few inches below the soil surface as soon as they emerge from the ground. Others say to let them grow to as high as 12 in. (30 cm). Some say what matters is time, not height, because the shoots grow tough and bitter when they are exposed to the sun for too long. I decided to harvest mine when they were no taller than 6 in. (15 cm); many were only 2 to 3 in. (5 to 7.5 cm) tall. I dug with my hori-hori to break the shoots about 1 in. (2.5 cm) below the soil surface.

In most cases I should have waited a day, or a few hours, anyway. There is not much to eat in a 2 in. (5 cm) tall, 1 in. (2.5 cm) wide bamboo shoot, after you remove all the sheath leaves. The skinniest shoots, ½ in. (1.25 cm) or less in diameter, were too much bother. I should have left those for the mower. The useful shoots were the thicker, taller ones.

All the bamboo experts seem to agree that bamboo shoots should be kept cool and cooked soon, so I collected mine over the course of just a week. I stored them in an unsealed plastic bag in the refrigerator.

As I washed and trimmed and peeled the shoots, I tasted many of them. They had an unpleasant rawness about them, but none were bitter, not even a few I'd harvested at 10 in. (25.5 cm) tall. I cut some 12 in. (30 cm) shoots and licked their ends; they weren't bitter, either. Later I discovered helpful advice in Daphne Lewis and Carol Miles's book *Farming Bamboo*: harvest the shoots at 6 to 12 in. (15 to 30 cm), for a maximum of tasty flesh without bitterness.

To make the shoots easy to peel, I scored them lengthwise, as you might an onion. I broke off the tips, which were all leaves without solid flesh, and trimmed off bottom ends that were damaged or very hard. Then, following instructions from Washington State University Extension, I cut the shoots crosswise into ⅛ in. (3.2 mm) rounds, some of them hollow and some of them solid, and boiled them in an uncovered pan of water for twenty minutes. Leaving the pan uncovered is supposed to allow the chemical that causes bitterness, hydrogen cyanide, to dissipate into the air (according to *Farming Bamboo*, tropical varieties are especially likely to contain cyanide-forming compounds). If any bitter taste remains in the shoots, boil them in fresh water for five minutes longer.

The initial twenty-minute cooking time was a compromise. Some Japanese writers call for as much as ninety minutes of boiling, always with rice bran added to remove bitterness, but in Japan cooks often boil their thick shoots whole. *Farming Bamboo* says that ten minutes of boiling is enough, and that non-bitter shoots can be added raw to stir-fries.

My cooked shoots weren't at all bitter. They were still firm to the tooth, but they had lost their raw taste. Their delicate flavor reminded me of artichoke bottoms.

How best to store cooked bamboo shoots? Japanese writers say to keep them covered with water in the refrigerator and to change the water every day; the shoots will keep this way for as long as a week. *Farming Bamboo* says that if you boil the shoots in lightly salted water, you can store them dry in a plastic bag or other container in the refrigerator. Again, I compromised, sort of: I'd boiled my shoots in unsalted water, but now I put them in a quart container and covered them with salted water (1 ½ teaspoons salt to 2 cups, or 473 mL, water). I figured I'd change the water every two or three days, adding a little salt each time.

Bamboo shoots can be frozen, too. If you slice and blanch them, says *Farming Bamboo*, you can store bamboo shoots in a sealed bag in a freezer for up to a year. They can go straight from the freezer into the wok. And you can pickle bamboo—in vinegar, with sugar and such flavorings as garlic and chile.

Besides providing a pleasant, mild flavor and an appealing crunch in salads and stir-fries, bamboo shoots are good for your health. They are low in calories, but they are high in potassium and fiber. That evening I briefly marinated two handfuls of bamboo shoots in a dressing of lemon juice and roasted hazelnut oil, and then I added the shoots to a salad of spinach, arugula, blanched asparagus, and sliced boiled eggs. A delicious way to celebrate springtime!

Spring Salad *with* Bamboo

SERVES 4

As with any mixed salad, you can vary the quantities and substitute ingredients as you please.

2 tablespoons lemon juice

Salt

¼ cup (60 mL) roasted hazelnut oil

2 handfuls prepared bamboo shoots

6 asparagus spears, cut into 2 in. (5 cm) lengths

1 bunch spinach, washed and dried

1 bunch arugula, washed and dried

4 eggs, boiled until the yolks are just firm,
    and peeled

1. In a small bowl, whisk together the lemon juice and salt to taste, and then whisk in the hazelnut oil. Add the bamboo shoots, turning them gently until they are covered with the dressing. Let the bowl stand while you assemble the rest of the salad.

2. Steam the asparagus or boil it in salted water until it is just tender, 2 to 3 minutes. Cool the asparagus in ice water, and drain.

3. Tear the spinach and arugula leaves into bite-size pieces, and mix them in a salad bowl. Drain the dressing from the bamboo shoots, and reserve it. Scatter the bamboo shoots and the asparagus pieces over the leaves. Slice the eggs into quarters, and lay the pieces on top of the salad. Drizzle the dressing over the salad, and serve.

Collards *for* Year-Round Greens

"**W**hat's this thing about kale?" asked a newbie in town, from Alabama, sipping her beer on a warm June evening on the terrace of our local brewpub. "I miss collards! Have you all ever even *heard* of collards?"

I had. I was growing them, thanks to a fellow gardener who had brought little hand-labeled envelopes of 'Yellow Cabbage' collard seeds to a seed swap.

I'd planted the seeds in the ground in late summer of the previous year, and the plants had grown slowly over the winter. Normally, if I plant brassicas too late for a fall harvest, they go to seed as soon as warm weather arrives, if they survive that long. But through the spring the collards grew lushly. By then I couldn't remember what I'd planted. I racked my brain to remember. These brassicas looked good enough to eat even in lettuce season, when we neglect other vegetables to stuff ourselves with sweet, tender lettuce before it turns milky and bitter.

By the time I met the Alabaman, the collard plants were 3 ft. (1 m) tall. And with scant watering they kept growing through the hot, dry summer. The plants were so beautiful that my husband asked me to plant some in the front yard, where the neighbors could admire them.

By the end of September, the tallest of my four collard plants was 4 ft. (1.2 m), and still the plants weren't going to seed. They bore big, open leaves all around the stem; the biggest leaves were 2 ft. (60 cm) long. I was picking forty snails off the leaves at a time—collard makes an excellent snail trap—but the snails were mostly eating the lower leaves, and the damage was scarcely noticeable from several feet away. The plants were still gorgeous.

We ate collard greens through the following winter, and the next spring the plants bloomed. This wasn't the end of them, however. I learned that collard is, or at least can be, perennial. When the plants get big, their stems tend to drop to the ground. When you cut off the top of the plant, a new top grows from the stem of the old one. This means that, if you've let a plant go to seed, you will have new ones ready to harvest by the time the old one has died. Before long you may have a big patch of collard. No wonder Southerners eat so much of this vegetable!

What exactly is collard? The plant is on the wilder side of the species *Brassica oleracea*, which includes head cabbage, cauliflower, broccoli, kale, kohlrabi, and Brussels sprouts (the word *collard* comes from *colewort*, an old name for wild cabbage). Like kale, collard is a cabbage that doesn't form a head. The thick green leaves have a waxy coating that repels water as oilcloth does. 'Tronchuda' cabbage, which Portuguese cooks slice for caldo verde, is a kind of collard; so are the greens that Brazilians serve as a side dish with feijoada. Collard is rich in manganese and vitamins A, C, and K.

In this country, collard isn't just a Southern food, although its association with poverty has dampened its popularity in the North. But the South has so many local varieties that a nonprofit organization, the Heirloom Collard Project (heirloomcollards.org), has formed to collect, study, and celebrate them.

'Yellow Cabbage' collard gets the *cabbage* part of its name because the plant makes a half-hearted effort at head formation, with small leaves in the center turning inward. The *yellow* part of the name makes sense when you've seen the dark blue-green color of many other collard varieties. 'Yellow Cabbage' is more of a yellow-green.

'Yellow Cabbage' collard got its start in Asheville, North Carolina, in 1887. There, Colonel Joe Branner developed collard with less bitter, thinner leaves and a yellower color than other collards had. Today the cultivar is grown mostly around Ayden, North Carolina, where Benny and Vickie Cox sell both bagged collard leaves and collard bedding plants from their roadside business, the Collard Shack. Ayden holds an annual collard festival, which includes a horseshoe tournament, the Dare Devil Dog Show, and a collard-eating contest.

In North Carolina, the harvest of spring-planted collard begins around Mother's Day. The leaves are considered best when they are young and small, no longer than 12 in. (30 cm). Although in general people prefer to eat collard when it has been sweetened by cold weather, 'Yellow Cabbage' is said to reach its peak flavor in mid-summer.

'Yellow Cabbage' collard seeds are available from Southern Exposure Seed Exchange. If you can't find 'Yellow Cabbage', I suggest trying any collard seeds you can get. Since first planting 'Yellow Cabbage' collard I've also grown the cultivar 'Georgia Southern', and it seems no more tough or bitter to me. Southern Exposure offers a dozen varieties of collard seed. And there are more: In their book *Collards: A Southern Tradition from Seed to Table*, Edward Davis and John Morgan describe sixty varieties that they collected across the South.

Once you've begun to harvest your collard greens, you can use them much as you might use kale. In the South, cut collard leaves are boiled with smoked or salted meat until the leaves are quite soft, for as long as two hours. But long cooking isn't necessary if you like greens with texture. You might simply sauté the cut leaves in oil, with garlic. Southerners sometimes use collard greens instead of head cabbage in sauerkraut. They also pickle collard in vinegar, with hot peppers and a little sugar. You can even make a massaged collard salad, which turns out very much like its kale counterpart.

Whether or not you've ever made massaged kale salad, you don't need a recipe for the collard version. First pick a few collard leaves—fewer than you think you'll need, because the leaves are surprisingly dense. Cut out the stems and slice the leaves into strips. Sprinkle some salt over the collard strips. Rub the strips with your fingers until they lose their waxy coating and turn bright green. Let them rest for about half an hour. Then taste the greens and rinse them if they are too salty. Now add lemon juice and other ingredients of your choice—pickled onions, sunflower or pumpkin seeds, black pepper, chunks of tomato, small pieces of fresh or dried fruit. Finally, toss in some olive oil. Eat.

You can also apply the salt-and-massage technique to collard greens you intend to cook; this will shorten the cooking time considerably. Let the massaged greens rest for thirty minutes before putting them over the heat.

Another good way to use collard leaves, my husband, Robert, and I discovered, is to make *patra*, an Indian dish of leaves filled with spiced chickpea paste, rolled, and fried. Although collard has no place in the traditional preparation, this variant is both practical in cooler climes and truly delicious. Here is the story behind the recipe.

When we were young and living in Somerville, Massachusetts, Robert and I liked to visit a tiny Indian market in Union Square. On one of our visits, he picked up a little can with a label picturing something dark green and golden brown, rolled and sliced like a cinnamon roll. Curious, we added the can to our pile of spices and legumes.

At home, we fried the rich, spicy, slightly sweet rolls, called patra, according to the instructions on the label. Every time we visited the store after that, we had to bring home patra.

Many years later, when an Indian salesman from Robert's company visited Oregon, he came to our house for dinner. Robert and I hadn't eaten patra in thirty-five years, but neither of us had forgotten its taste. So in the talk of Indian foods Robert asked about patra. Ankur was surprised. The women in his family used to make it, but they hadn't in recent years. Ankur hadn't tasted patra in a long time.

Ankur was no cook, so he couldn't tell us how to make patra. But he knew we needed a special leaf, a big leaf. He tried and tried but couldn't remember the English name of the plant.

Knowing how enthusiastically Indian cooks have taken to the Internet, I later googled "patra recipe." Suddenly, patra lost all its mystery. The big leaf, I learned, is from taro, or colocasia, as Indians prefer to call it; the Hindi name is *arbi ke patte*. This is the tropical wetland plant whose starchy tubers are a staple food for Pacific Islanders and West Indians (the latter call the plant dasheen). Taro's arrow-shaped leaves are edible, says one Indian writer, only when they "are not itchy"—that is, when the variety is low in calcium oxalate, which causes itching in the mouth and throat. The paste around which the leaves are wrapped is made up mostly of *besan*, gram flour—or, to us, chickpea or garbanzo flour.

Some cool-climate gardeners grow taro in summer and dig up the tubers in fall to overwinter indoors, but I have no patience for ever-thirsty plants, especially when they can't survive the winter outdoors. And I'm sure that no grocery store in this town stocks colocasia leaves. Still, Robert wasn't discouraged. He figured he'd just found a new use for collard leaves. The next day Robert studied several patra recipes on the Internet and created his own.

The spices covered up the cabbagy flavor so well that Robert's collard patra tasted, to us, just like the taro version we remembered from the Indian market. Robert took a picture of his patra and sent it to Ankur. About a week later, Ankur sent back a very similar picture of a dish from his own family meal. Apparently, he had talked his wife or mother into making patra—with taro leaves, of course.

Collard Patra

MAKES ABOUT 3 DOZEN

Although patra may look like an appetizer or side dish, it is very nourishing. With the sole addition of sautéed daylily buds, collard patra made a lovely dinner for Robert and me.

3 medium collard leaves

1 ½ cups (180 g) chickpea flour

1 teaspoon ground dried hot pepper

2 teaspoons ground coriander

1 teaspoon ground cumin

2 tablespoons brown sugar

About ½ teaspoon salt

One 1 in. (2.5 cm) slice fresh ginger, chopped

1 green jalapeño pepper, seeded and chopped

6 small garlic cloves, chopped

About ⅔ cup (158 mL) water

Oil, for frying

1 tablespoon brown mustard seeds

2 teaspoons sesame seeds

1 small bunch cilantro, chopped

1. Cut the large central rib out of the collard leaves, and then cut each leaf in half lengthwise. Trim each leaf half into a rectangular shape. With a rolling pin, lightly crush each leaf half to make it more pliable.

2. Combine the flour, pepper, coriander, cumin, sugar, and salt in a bowl. In a mortar or food processor, make a paste of the ginger, jalapeño, and garlic. Add the paste to the flour mixture, and stir well. Add water a little at a time, stirring, until the mixture forms a spreadable paste.

3. Lay a leaf half on a board. Spread some of the paste in a thin layer on top. Place a second leaf half over the first, and spread the paste in a thin layer over the top. Roll the leaf halves to form a log. Use the rest of the leaf halves and paste to make two more logs in the same way.

4. Place the logs in a steamer heated to a boil. (Robert uses a Chinese bamboo steamer set over a wok.) Steam the patra for 25 minutes.

5. Let the logs cool. Slice them crosswise into ⅜ to ½ in. (1 to 1.25 cm) rounds.

6. Pour enough oil into a large skillet to cover the bottom ¼ in. (0.5 cm) deep. Turn the heat to medium. When the oil is hot, add the mustard and sesame seeds. As soon as the seeds begin popping, place a single layer of patra rounds in the pan. Cook until the paste begins to brown, about 1 minute. Turn the rounds, cooking them on the other side for about 1 minute longer. Transfer them to a dish lined with paper towels to soak up the excess oil. Cook the remaining slices in the same way.

7. Serve the patra warm with a sprinkling of cilantro.

Blue-Fruited Honeysuckle

*I*f you've come upon fruiting blue honeysuckle bushes in your local garden center this year, you can thank two fruit-loving Oregonians, Jim Gilbert and Maxine Thompson.

After one of his fruit-gathering trips to Russia in the 1990s, Jim introduced American gardeners to *Lonicera caerulea*—or the honeyberry, as he called it—through his mail-order nursery, One Green World. Later Maxine, a professor emeritus in horticulture at Oregon State University, began breeding the Japanese subspecies, from the northern island of Hokkaido. Maxine called the berries haskap, their Ainu name. She sold plants of numbered selections to people who wanted to test them and, subsequently, propagation rights to nurseries around the world.

If you choose the right variety for your region, these plants may be worth a try in your garden. Dark-skinned, with a bloom, the fruits look like elongated blueberries. They are high in vitamin C and richer in antioxidants than even black currants. The berries are not particularly aromatic, but they are mildly sweet and moderately to strongly tart. Their many seeds are hardly noticeable on the tongue. The berries make a luscious jam with no need for added pectin and none of the graininess of blueberry jam.

I planted two of Jim's honeyberry varieties on our Scio farm about fifteen years ago. One never produced berries; the other yielded a few, but only once or twice. I admit that I probably didn't water the plants often enough, but Maxine, when I visited her homestead in wooded hills north of Corvallis, explained to me the bigger problem: The two Russian subspecies, *Lonicera caerulea* var. *edulis* and *L. caerulea* var. *kamtschatica*, are adapted to extremely cold winters. Here in the Willamette Valley, they break dormancy too early and as a result bloom too early. The Japanese subspecies, *L. caerulea* var. *emphyllocalyx*, blooms about a month later.

And yet haskaps are the earliest berries of the year, ripening even before strawberries.

The three plants Maxine sold me, each of a different numbered variety, grew into little vase-shaped shrubs beside our farmhouse. They looked very different from the sprawling honeyberry plants I'd bought from One Green World. One of those was entirely prostrate and the other a little taller, but both seemed unsure whether they were vine or bush.

Upon selling the farm I said goodbye to Jim's honeyberries, dug up Maxine's plants, and set the haskaps in our little city garden, where they have thrived. Now more than ten years old, they are 4 to 5 ft. (1.2 to 1.5 m) tall. Each year, they produce more fruit than I can pick. I haven't weighed my crops, but the average haskap bush, after the first five years, is said to produce 8 to 10 lb. (3.6 to 4.5 kg) of fruit.

As Maxine must have intended, my three selections together exemplify the diversity among haskaps. The fruits of one bush are long and torpedo-shaped, extra tart, and least numerous. The more productive, medium-size plant has thick, blunt-ended, sweeter berries. The smallest plant has the shortest berries, and their tendency to hold on to their blossoms makes for a bit of fuss in the kitchen.

The *Lonicera caerulea* plants you find in your garden center will have names, not numbers. Yezberries (Yez is an old name for Hokkaido) are Maxine's selections, released in 2016 and 2017. Yezberries 'Maxie', 'Solo', 'Keiko', 'Tana', 'Taka', 'Kawai', and 'Willa' all bloom late and are suitable for warmer climates, like mine. 'Strawberry Sensation' from Berries Unlimited, with its strawberry-like aftertaste, is also late-blooming. Early-, mid-, and late-blooming varieties have been developed by Bob Bors of the University of Saskatchewan by crossing

Maxine's Japanese selections with Russian honeyberries. Bob's releases include the late bloomers 'Boreal Blizzard' and 'Boreal Beauty' and, for colder regions, the earlier-blooming Indigo series, 'Indigo Gem', 'Tundra', 'Borealis', 'Aurora', and 'Honeybee'. Another early bloomer is 'Berry Smart', bred in the Czech Republic. (You'll find information on all of these at the Honeyberry USA website, honeyberryusa.com.)

None of these haskap or honeyberry varieties is self-fruitful, so plan to buy at least two plants, of different, compatible varieties. Plant them 5 to 6 ft. (1.5 to 1.8 m) apart in a sunny place; most will grow 4 to 6 ft. (1.2 to 1.8 m) tall and nearly as wide. Mulch around the base of each plant.

After planting, haskaps require little care. Water them now and then, but don't worry—they aren't nearly as thirsty as blueberries. *Lonicera caerulea* doesn't need acidic soil, either. After four or five years you'll probably want to prune the bushes lightly, by removing weak growth and the oldest wood; this will make harvest easier.

You'll probably be harvesting more than once each season, because the berries don't ripen all at once. Some varieties hold on to their fruits better than others, making it possible to delay the harvest. Picking is time-consuming, so you might want to lay a sheet under the bush and shake it, though I haven't tried this. Perhaps better yet, recruit some children to help pick.

Like many plants new to a region, haskaps and honeyberries at first seemed pest-free in North America. Just last year, however, I noticed that my haskaps had a serious problem with borers. I haven't yet seen the critters, so I don't know the species, but for now I'm cutting out all damaged stems. For the past few years, too, my haskaps have been plagued by spotted-wing drosophila, the fruit fly that destroys barely ripe fruit. They make the berries mushy, and, if you squeeze one, juice will leak out of one or more tiny holes. To keep away the fruit flies next year, I may cover the bushes, after they flower, with fine netting. At a minimum I'll cover the ground around the bushes with black plastic sheeting, to keep the larvae from pupating in the soil.

Haskap berries are easy to store and prepare, as Maxine assured me. They need no seeding, stemming, or peeling. An octogenarian fireball when I met her—she died in 2021, at ninety-five—Maxine was freezing most of her berries

and sending each of her buyers home with a bag of frozen fruit and a recipe for haskap crisp. The berries serve just as well in a pie or a jam. And with their tart taste and strong color, they make a lovely chutney too.

Haskap Chutney

MAKES ABOUT 1 PINT (473 mL)

This chutney is much like jam, but cooked slower, with added flavorings. It is not intended to gel, though it should turn out rather thick. The apple chunks provide a textural contrast to the jammy berries (be sure to select a variety that keeps its shape, such as 'Honeycrisp' or 'Golden Delicious'). I've used brown mustard, the traditional mustard seeds of India, but I think I'd like yellow ones even more, because they are bigger and more noticeable on the tongue. You might serve this chutney with roasted or grilled pork or chicken.

2 teaspoons mustard oil or other vegetable oil

1 ½ teaspoons mustard seeds

½ teaspoon fennel seeds

½ teaspoon cumin seeds

1 pound (454 g) haskaps

1 medium apple (about 5 oz. or 140 g), peeled, cored, and diced large

⅔ cup (140 g) brown sugar

3 tablespoons cider vinegar

2 teaspoons grated fresh ginger

1 ½ teaspoons hot pepper flakes

¼ teaspoon salt, plus more as needed

1. Heat the oil over medium heat in a medium saucepan. Add the mustard, fennel, and cumin seeds, and heat them until they begin popping. Stir in the haskaps, apple, brown sugar, vinegar, ginger, pepper flakes, and salt. Gently boil the mixture, stirring occasionally, until it is as thick as hot jam, about 30 minutes.

2. When the chutney has cooled, store it in the refrigerator.

Strawberries *from the* Woods

T he first time I planted alpine strawberries, I set them under the arching canes of an old climbing rose. They seemed to relish the long, wet spring that followed. The pale pink roses, white from a distance, were just beginning to bloom when I tasted the first just-ripe berries. Breathing in the combined fragrance of the roses and strawberries, I dreamed of my jam pot.

The strawberries were 'Alexandria', a seed-propagated cultivar of *Fragaria vesca* var. *semperflorens* (or *F. vesca* var. *vesca* ssp. *semperflorens*, or *F. alpina*) introduced by Park Seed in 1964. *F. vesca* is the woodland strawberry, a species of small-fruited plants native to North America, Europe, and western Asia. Its cultivation—and the cultivation of strawberries in general—began in the 1300s, when Europeans started transplanting runners from the woods to their gardens. The plant was at first appreciated more as an ornamental, flowering groundcover than as a source of fruit, but some people collected and ate the little berries. Strawberries were sold by London street vendors by 1430, and in 1526 *The Grete Herball* identified them as helpful for the choleric and the dyspeptic. By the late 1500s they were a popular addition to English, French, and Italian gardens, and the berries were "eaten with Creame and Sugar" for "a greate refreshing to men," and, most beneficially for the choleric, "with Wine and Sugar."

Today these strawberries might not impress us. But in 1532 a superior variety was described, one that grew in the Alps. It grew vigorously and began

flowering only three to four months after germination, and then continued flowering and fruiting until winter. The plant wasn't widely shared among gardeners, however, until it was rediscovered in the 1760s. By this time the breeding of the big modern strawberry (*Fragaria xananassa*) had begun, but alpines remained the strawberries of choice for French gardeners well into the nineteenth century. (Thomas Jefferson appreciated them, too; he first sowed them in 1774, and twenty years later he told James Monroe that they were one of the "three objects which you should endeavor to enrich our country with.")

Today alpine strawberries are still prized, at least in France. They top little custard tarts and Belgian waffles; they are served in stemmed glasses with crème fraîche; and, classically, they are combined with red wine and sugar. American gardeners may use them in similar ways or just delight in sampling them when passing by the little plants.

Alpine strawberries are distinctive. They tend to be larger than other woodland strawberries, but they are tiny in comparison with today's commercial monsters: Alpines are no more than 1 in. (2.5 cm) long. They are narrow and pointed, not round or heart shaped. Their skin is usually red—sometimes pale red, or almost orange—but it can also be yellow or white. (White skin seems to be a common mutation; at least one seedling of my 'Alexandria' bore white fruit. Conversely, seedlings of white varieties sometimes produce red fruit.) Inside, their flesh is soft and white.

Alpine strawberries taste sweet and have an intense strawberry fragrance. Some people also detect hints of rose or vanilla. There is a touch of pineapple, which is magnified in the yellow and white varieties. Eating a perfectly ripe berry brings a shocking rush of flavor. No matter how jaded you are from crunching gigantic, green-picked strawberries from California, you will recognize the alpine flavor as the essence of strawberry.

The plant's appearance is also distinctive. Although some varieties produce runners, most produce few or none. The plants grow in tidy clumps that expand by increasing their root mass, but never greatly. The dark green leaves are deeply veined. Alpine strawberries look good lining a border or growing in pots.

One special characteristic of alpine strawberries is that they are day-neutral—that is, they fruit all through the growing season, from June until frost. This means that unless you have a big plot your harvest will always be small, but it will be continuous.

Various cultivars of alpine strawberries are available, usually in seed form. 'Alexandria' is valued for its high production, fast growth, and good germination. The standard commercial variety in Europe is 'Reine des Vallées'. Currently I'm growing 'Mignonette', an improved cultivar of 'Reine des Vallées' that may be somewhat less hardy and productive but is said to be the best tasting of the reds. 'Déesse des Vallées' ("Goddess of the Valleys") is another improved version of 'Reine des Vallées'. Other red varieties are German in origin: 'Ruegen' (or 'Rügen'), 'Waldsteinchen', and 'Bowlenzauber'. 'Attila' is a trailing type; 'Golden Alexandria' has golden to light green leaves. Yellow-fruited alpine strawberries include 'Holiday' (from Estonia) and 'Yellow Wonder'. White alpines are said to be especially sweet and to fool the birds, who are more attracted to red. White cultivars include 'Ivory', 'Milk', 'White Solemacher', and 'White Soul'. 'Pineapple Crush' is intermediate in color between the whites and yellows, and some prize it as the most flavorful of all the alpine strawberries.

Alpine strawberries are easy to grow. They like fertile soil and plenty of sun, though they benefit from afternoon shade in hot regions. They prefer not to be crowded, so set them about 18 in. (46 cm) apart. Mulching is a good idea, since consistent soil moisture encourages fruit production. But these are relatively tough plants; they will tolerate short periods of drought.

Starting the plants from seed takes patience; you need to chill the seeds for three to four weeks before sowing, and then the seeds may take as long as six weeks to sprout. But if you start with a little nursery plant it will probably self-sow readily. Nature will do the work of propagation for you.

You can divide your plants after a year or two. After three years they will definitely need division to maintain good production. Divide your clump into two to four pieces (no more) and reset them.

On that early summer day under the rose bower, I collected a couple of handfuls of berries and then looked up at the roses. I hadn't yet made rose preserves that year, and I'd missed the peak bloom of both the rugosas and the delicate pink wild roses. But I knew I could find enough roses to combine with the strawberries. The flowers overhead were too pale for a red jam, sadly. For better color and an equally delicious aroma, I collected some pink moss roses, pulling the blossoms away from each calyx with one hand and, with the other, clipping off each petal's pale, slightly bitter base with the tiny scissors of my pocketknife.

Then I remembered the rhubarb stalks I'd harvested a few hours earlier. Rhubarb can be problematic for preservers and bakers because it is typically ambivalent about color. The varieties that are red inside and out tend to lack vigor, and all-green varieties are hard to find. Most rhubarb in home gardens has red or red-speckled skin but green flesh, and even red rhubarb skin may lose much of its color in the wrong growing conditions. The color problem is one reason that rhubarb is so often combined with strawberries.

The happy marriage of flavors is another reason; the tartness of the rhubarb complements the sweet perfume of the strawberries. But full-scented roses marry well with rhubarb and strawberry both, so why not a ménage à trois? This I had to try.

Rhubarb–Rose–Alpine Strawberry Jam

MAKES ABOUT 1 ½ PINTS (710 mL)

To smell and to eat, this jam is fantastic—it captures June in a jar. You don't need to use packaged pectin in this jam. It is thickened by natural pectin in the strawberries and rhubarb and by insoluble fiber in the rhubarb.

1 pound (454 g) rhubarb, cut crosswise ½ in. (1.25 cm) thick

3 ounces (85 g) alpine strawberries (about ¾ cup)

2 ½ ounces (71 g) fragrant, unsprayed red or pink rose petals (about 1 ½ cups, well packed)

1 tablespoon lemon juice

2 cups (400 g) sugar

1. Gently mix the rhubarb, strawberries, rose petals, lemon juice, and sugar in a large bowl. Cover the bowl, and let it sit at room temperature for about 8 hours, until the sugar has mostly dissolved.

2. Pour the mixture into a preserving pan, and set the pan over medium heat. Stir gently. When the sugar is completely dissolved, raise the heat to medium-high. Boil, stirring occasionally. The mixture will thicken in just a few minutes as the rhubarb fibers separate. When the mixture has reached a jam-like consistency, remove the pan from the heat. Ladle the jam into jars, and close them.

3. You can process the jars in a boiling-water bath, if you like, for 5 minutes if you have sterilized them or 10 minutes if you haven't.

Walnuts, Green *and* Ripe

I've never had my own producing English walnut tree. Planting a walnut is practical only if you have a very large parcel, for the trees can grow to 50 ft. (15 m) tall and wide. They shade the area beneath the crown, discouraging sun-loving plants, and anyhow you want to keep that area clear to make harvesting easier.

If you do plant a walnut tree, you will have to wait a long time to gather nuts. The trees take about ten years to come into full production. My father planted a walnut in our backyard when I was about eight, and when I left for college at seventeen it had not produced a single nut. I myself planted a walnut tree on our farm, and then I cut it down, before it reached bearing age, when we installed solar panels on the roof of the garage, just to the north of the tree.

Thankfully, it's easy to forage for walnuts, at least here in western Oregon. I start in late June, on or about St. John's Day, the 24th of June. This is the traditional day in Europe to harvest green walnuts.

If you live in the country, you begin your foray simply by walking the rural roads. After a while you'll look up into the great green canopy of an old tree that somehow survived the destruction, by storm or bulldozer, of a once-lucrative orchard, or that once shaded a farmhouse that has long since crumbled or

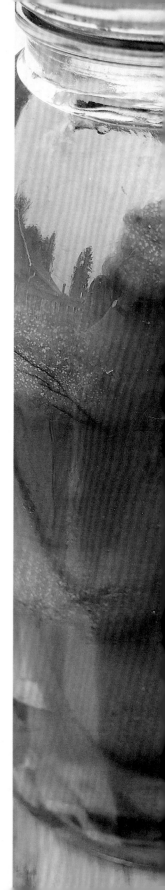

burned. If you're unsure that the tree is a walnut—English, not black—kick the dirt at your feet, and uncover an old half shell or a whole nut, speckled with mold. Scan the branches for bright green fruits, oval and no more than 2 in. (5 cm) long (if the nuts are much smaller, come back later; in Oregon they sometimes aren't ready to harvest until mid-July). If the tree is at the edge of a grass or grainfield, with no occupied house nearby, the farmer is almost surely absentee. He, or she, would be happy to have you take some nuts, and probably the rest of the tree with them. Fill your pockets. Promise the tree you'll be back come fall, to pick mature nuts off the ground.

If you live in a city, as I do now, you may still find walnut trees along the streets. My neighborhood, in fact, used to have a commercial walnut orchard. Most of the trees were lost in the 1962 Columbus Day storm, which pretty well finished the Willamette Valley's walnut industry. A lone tree that came down on a neighbor's house was pulled upright and held in place by a cable attached to a deadman, an underground anchor. Both the cable and the deadman are still in place, and the old tree is thriving and productive. Other individual trees survived as well, often in roadside planting strips. Some of them, long ago grafted on black walnut rootstock, now have black walnut foliage and nuts on some branches, and English walnut foliage and nuts on other branches. Most of the trees, though, were planted from seed, by humans or squirrels. For this reason, their nuts vary—in size, flavor, shell thickness, and tendency to shed or hang on to their husks. In the fall we find the better nuts—especially, the ones that shed their husks—and pick them up in the street or ask permission to harvest from a neighbor's front yard. The answer is almost always yes. A single walnut tree, after all, can provide plenty of nuts for several families. The challenge with green nuts is finding some that you can reach, since street trees are usually pruned high.

Wherever you find your green walnuts, hold one to your nose as you walk, to inhale the delicious resinous aroma—a cross, to my nose, between lime and eucalyptus. Too bad a green walnut isn't edible, not in its natural state. But you can make it so, provided the nut hasn't yet developed a hard shell. To be sure you've harvested in time, pierce one of the nuts with a needle when you get home. You should be able to easily push the needle to the center.

Before eating the nuts, you'll want to soak out their bitterness in multiple changes of water. Then you can either pickle them or preserve them in syrup. Pickled walnuts are, for me, interesting at best, but I love spicy, syrupy, chewy

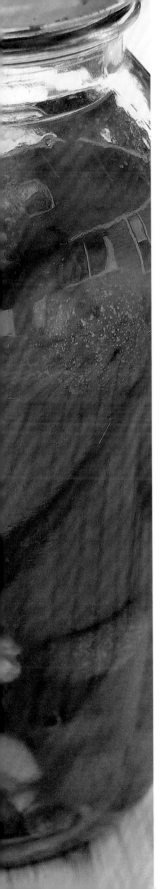

walnut preserves, especially for the way the peeled green fruits take on the brain-like shape of mature, hulled walnuts. My *Joy of Pickling* includes a recipe for pickled walnuts, and my *Joy of Jams, Jellies, and Other Sweet Preserves* has one for green walnut preserves.

You don't need to soak your walnuts if you plan to drink them—that is, to drink in their bitter taste and perfume in an alcoholic beverage. You need only about two dozen green walnuts to make a liter of green walnut liqueur. Called *liqueur de noix* by the French, *licor de nueces verdes* by Spaniards, *orahovac* by Croats, and, most famously, *nocino* or *nocillo* by Italians, the liqueur is made by simply steeping fresh, unhusked green walnuts with a few other flavorings in alcohol.

"It tastes like Christmas," two of my children told me, on separate occasions, upon first tasting green walnut liqueur. Sip the liqueur in winter as an aperitif or nightcap, perhaps with milk or cream, or dilute it with white wine for a warm-weather drink.

When you return to your tree in autumn to collect fallen nuts, don't put them into buckets and forget about them. You must remove any clinging pieces of husk, especially if the nuts are wet from rain, and then spread the nuts in a warm, dry place. We use our basement pool table, covered for its protection, and leave the basement windows open when the weather is warm. A heater or fan or both can be helpful but usually aren't necessary.

When the nuts are thoroughly dry, crack and store them as soon as possible, before any insect eggs can hatch. I use a hand-cranked Davebilt nutcracker, which cracks nuts as they enter the hopper between two big steel disks. But my friend Betty, whose one big, prolific walnut tree provides her with a seasonal business, cracks all her nuts with just a hammer. Neither of us can avoid the laborious job of sorting the nuts from the shells, but this is a fine occupation for winter nights, while you're listening to stories or watching (not too intently) a movie. Pack the walnuts in freezer bags or other airtight containers and store them, if possible, in a freezer, where any stray insect eggs will die, and rancidity will not develop. The nuts will easily keep well for two years.

I shouldn't ignore here the black walnut, which has its own virtues. Most important, its wood is handsome, hard, and tough, and suitable for furniture and carving as well as lumber. Many people value the tree's strong-flavored nuts as well—so much so that they manage to remove the husks (often by driving a car over the nuts on a graveled driveway), to break the hard, round

shells, and to fastidiously pick out the meats. Despite all this difficulty, black walnuts have been, and still are, a commercial product. I remember black walnut and cherry ice cream from my childhood.

But we never used the nuts from the black walnut tree on our farm. Instead, we would always find a source for English walnuts. I greatly wish that cities and counties would plant English walnuts on public land, so that more people could have a crack at the harvest.

Green Walnut Liqueur

MAKES ABOUT 4 ¼ CUPS (1 L)

This recipe is much like most others of its kind, except that I use honey in place of the usual refined sugar. The larger amount of sweetener is more traditional, but Robert and I like our liqueur less sweet. Occasional additions are vanilla beans (perhaps to imitate the effect of aging in oak, which is sometimes done for commercial walnut liqueurs), orange peel, and walnut leaves. The alcohol can be in the form of brandy, marc, or eau-de-vie instead of vodka.

1 pound (454 g) green walnuts (about 24)

One 3 in. (7.5 cm) cinnamon stick

6 cloves

Zest of 1 lemon, in strips

¾ to 1 ½ cups (255 to 510 g) honey

4 ¼ cups (1 L) vodka

1. Wearing gloves so your hands don't blacken, crack each walnut by smacking it with the side of a heavy knife or cleaver. Don't worry if some nuts break into pieces. Put the nuts in an 8 cup (2 L) jar along with the cinnamon, cloves, and lemon zest. Pour the honey over the nut mixture. Add the vodka, close the jar tightly, and shake it briefly. Wash your cutting board immediately so the walnut juice doesn't blacken it.

2. Every day, shake the jar or stir its contents. This not only helps the honey dissolve but also turns the nuts so that contact with air will eventually blacken them all over. When this happens, you can put the jar in a cupboard. The liquid will turn nearly black, and the walnuts will sink to the bottom.

3. At least 2 months after mixing the ingredients, filter the liquid through muslin (some years I take several months to get around to this, but no matter). The liqueur will be as black as strong coffee, with a slight greenish tinge. Funnel the liqueur into bottles, close them tightly, and store them in a dark place for as long as you like. Many people say that green walnut liqueur is best after aging for a year.

Sour Sorrel

O n the farm I made the mistake of creating a rhubarb bed by laying stacks of newspapers on top of the soil and covering them with mint pomace, a byproduct of the local industry of peppermint distillation. Mint pomace—or "pummy," in local parlance—is an excellent soil amendment, rich in nitrogen. But the newspaper stacks were too thick to break down, even after two or three years, and the cotton strings with which I'd tied them seemed imperishable. My rhubarb grew well enough in this bed, but even happier among the newspaper stacks was sheep sorrel, or field sorrel, or *Rumex acetosella*. Sheep sorrel is a weed, imported from Eurasia, with fast-spreading rhizomatous roots that are so thin and easily broken—especially when they are tangled with cotton string—that the plant is very difficult to eradicate.

I didn't mind. In past years I had grown *Rumex scutatus*, also known as French sorrel and buckler sorrel, which has larger, shield-shaped leaves. But that delicate species never survived the winter in our saturated clay soil. For the time being, sheep sorrel was an adequate substitute. Since the sheep sorrel grew no more than a few inches high it couldn't compete with rhubarb, its much larger cousin in the family Polygonaceae. And whenever the sheep sorrel grew too vigorously or began to set seed, I would pull up the plants, removing as much of the creeping roots as I could and taking the leaves into the house to make into soup.

Soon after we moved to town, I dug all the grass from the planting strip in front of the house, covered the soil with plastic sheeting for several weeks to kill seeds and pests, and then planted various shrubs and perennials. Seeds of a few weeds survived, mostly sweet violet, which I love, but also, in a small patch, sheep sorrel. Now I had no patience with the sorrel. I began regularly grubbing it out. Nine years later, I am still trying to get rid of it.

I have spurned my once-valued weed because I no longer need it. In the backyard, among my very first plantings was another sorrel—*Rumex acetosa*, also known as garden sorrel or English sorrel.

Garden sorrel is arguably more French than English. The French have been improving it from the wild species since the late 1600s. The oldest named variety is 'Large de Belleville', which is probably what I had planted—and am still growing—though the pot it came in was labeled simply *sorrel*. Other French cultivars are 'Blonde de Lyon', presumably lighter green in color, and 'Verte de Nonay'. 'Large' is probably the tallest of these three, but in general they all grow to about 2 ft. (60 cm), compared to the 6 to 12 in. (15 to 30 cm) that French sorrel reaches. Garden sorrel is also more tart than French sorrel.

A newer, patented cultivar of *Rumex acetosa* is 'Profusion', introduced in Canada in 1993. 'Profusion' doesn't flower or produce seeds at all, and so must be propagated through division or cuttings. It is said to have wide, tender, dark green leaves and to grow in neat mounds. I haven't seen this cultivar in Oregon yet.

There are many other species of *Rumex*, a genus that includes dock as well as sorrel. Among them is the very ornamental wood dock, bloody dock, or *R. sanguineus*. Its lime-green, red-veined leaves grow to about 18 in. (46 cm). They can be eaten when young, but this is a species better for looking at than eating. It also seems to me much thirstier and less hardy than garden sorrel.

Garden sorrel, then, is the sorrel that now supplies my kitchen. It is a long-lived perennial that thrives in full sun or semi-shade. With regular water it produces generously, but the plant can grow happily through the dry season with only occasional irrigation. Even in cold regions sorrel doesn't die, because it is hardy to -20°F (-29°C). In my climate, the leaves are usable year-round. I harvest the younger, smaller, more tender leaves, especially if I am adding them to a salad or sandwich, but the older leaves are also good, provided they are cooked. Cutting down the seed stalks when they appear encourages more leaf production, though you might prefer to let the plant go to seed; if the rain falls or you apply water at the right time, you will have baby plants to share. You can also multiply your sorrel plants by dividing them in spring, after they are two or three years old.

Like rhubarb, all species of *Rumex* are rich in oxalic acid, which gives the leaves their sour, lemon-like flavor. These species are not to be confused, however, with clover-like *Oxalis*, or wood sorrels, although *Oxalis* species, too, are edible. California children love to chew the stems of a yellow-flowered wood sorrel, *O. stricta*, which they call sourgrass (it is native not to California but to eastern North America and Asia). According to Patience Gray, author of *Honey from a Weed*, the French once considered *Oxalis* the best sorrel for *potage Germiny*—sorrel soup thickened with egg yolks—which even today typically bears a garnish of slivered French or garden sorrel in imitation of tiny wood sorrel stems, for the stems didn't break down with pounding as the leaves did.

With a name that comes from the same root as *sour*, sorrel has a long history as both a medicinal and a culinary herb. It has been considered cooling and cleansing, a remedy for liver, bladder, and kidney problems (although those prone to stones are advised to limit their consumption or to consume sorrel cooked but not raw). The water in which sorrel has been boiled is traditionally used as a skin wash and drunk with honey for fever and sinus infections. Over much of Europe, sorrel has been a traditional ingredient in green sauces, made with cream and butter in France and mixed herbs and sour milk or cream in Germany, and served with meat or fish. Not only does sorrel's acidity complement protein-rich foods, but the leaves, without their stems, break down without pounding or straining. Europeans have also used sorrel as a stuffing for river fish (it is supposed to dissolve the little bones), as an acidifying addition to spinach soup, and, sautéed in butter, as an accompaniment to steamed potatoes, veal, eggs, and poultry. Such dishes were once popular in North America, too, although sorrel hasn't yet regained the popularity here that it lost with the industrialization of our food system.

The cook preparing sorrel for the first time should remember three things: (1) You must use nonreactive cookware with this acidic vegetable. (2) Sorrel needs only very brief cooking. (3) Sorrel won't keep its bright color with cooking. Heat turns the leaves army green.

To preserve the greenness of sorrel-based dishes, you can combine the sorrel with other green vegetables. I have often made sorrel soups with chopped scallions or leeks instead of bulb onions (and I usually thicken the soup with potato instead of egg). The soup turns out not gray-green but moss green, a much more appetizing color. For an even greener soup, I set some of the sorrel leaves aside, cook the soup and let it cool briefly, and then add the rest of the leaves when I purée the soup in the blender.

Green Sorrel Soup

SERVES 2 AS A MAIN DISH, 4 AS A STARTER

This soup is warming on a cool evening, but you can also serve it cold. If that's your plan, let the cooked ingredients cool well before you blend them with the cream and raw sorrel leaves. Chill the soup for at least several hours.

3 tablespoons (42 g) butter

5 cups (1.2 L) chopped scallions or leeks

4 cups (1 L) chicken stock

1 medium-large russet potato, peeled and diced

8 cups (2 L) stemmed sorrel leaves, loosely packed

1 cup (237 mL) cream

Salt

1. Melt the butter in a nonreactive pot. Add the scallions to the butter and gently cook until they are tender.

2. Add the stock. When it has nearly begun to boil, add the potato. Cover the pot and cook until the potato pieces are tender, about 15 minutes.

3. Set aside some of the most tender sorrel leaves, about a quarter of the total. Stir the rest of the sorrel leaves into the pot. As soon as they have wilted, remove the pot from the heat. Let the pot stand, uncovered, for about 5 minutes. Then whirl the mixture until smooth in a blender, in batches, if needed. Take care to begin on low speed and turn up the speed gradually. Blend in the cream, add salt to taste, and then blend in the remaining raw sorrel leaves. Serve the soup immediately.

4. If needed, you can reheat the soup before serving, although the green color will dull.

Kale Buds *and* Collard Tops

About the time you get tired of eating collard or kale leaves (see "Collards for Year-Round Greens"), the plants may begin to bolt. What do you do now? Keep eating!

Years ago, I discovered how good kale florets taste. Along with the thin, flexible stem tips that bear them, they are sweet, tender, and not at all bitter. You can eat the little attached leaves as well, because although kale leaves get smaller as they rise up the stalk, they don't grow tough and bitter like bolting lettuce.

When I started growing collard, I found that collard florets tasted even better than kale florets. Collards and kales form their buds at about the same time, in mid-March to early April in western Oregon. The wonderful thing about collard florets is that the top 6 in. (15 cm) or so of each stem is sweet, tender, and not at all bitter. So, although I call kale florets buds, with collard I cut long, asparagus-like pieces from the top of the plant and call them collard *tops* rather than buds.

After the initial cuts, kale and collard will continue trying to flower. This means I can harvest a second crop and perhaps a third, with the tops a little shorter each time. Eventually I let the plants produce their flowers, because the honeybees are grateful for this early-season forage. Besides, most years I want to collect some seed after the flowering has finished.

I must admit at this point that I strongly dislike broccoli. Broccoli is much hailed as the world's most healthful food, as if no other brassicas existed besides broccoli, head cabbage, and cauliflower. Broccoli slows damage from osteoarthritis! It detoxifies air pollutants! It helps prevent cancer! Certainly, broccoli is good for you, but there is little unique about it. After all, head cabbage, cauliflower, kale, collard, Brussels sprouts, kohlrabi, and gai lan are all *Brassica oleracea*, the same species as broccoli. Yet scientists have devoted much research to figuring out how to get children to willingly eat only those little green "trees" that we call broccoli.

The problem with broccoli, the pundits say, is that it is bitter. And it is, slightly, but not nearly so bitter as other vegetables that children accept more readily, such as carrots. Broccoli certainly doesn't compare in bitterness to some varieties of broccoli rabe (*Brassica rapa* Broccoletto group), also known as broccoli raab, rapini, and broccoletti. Broccoli rabe can be truly bitter. I grew it once and tore the plant out; to me it was inedible.

Some scientists have noticed the sulfurous stink of broccoli and other brassicas. This stink is produced through long cooking, but researchers have found that it also occurs through chewing, even when the vegetable is raw. Chewing these brassicas activates an enzyme that breaks down a chemical in the vegetables that thereby releases pungent odor molecules. One of these compounds is also produced by rotting meat. In some people's saliva, perhaps because of bacteria in their mouths, much more of this stinky compound arises. Kids whose chewing produces more of the offensive volatiles hate cauliflower the most, a study found. Presumably these children would hate broccoli as much as cauliflower.

What the researchers ignore, however, is the *texture* of broccoli. I eat broccoli stems happily—although, unlike kale and collard stems, they usually must be peeled. But the heads? The feel of all those little bumps on the tongue is, to me, unpleasant. With cooking the texture worsens; then I'm tasting mushy little bumps. I'm sure I'm not alone in this distaste.

Perhaps one thing superior about kale and collard is that the florets are smaller. You don't feel as many little buds on the tongue at once. And at the same time, you taste plenty of sweet, crunchy stem.

Kale and collard florets are wonderful when simply sautéed with garlic and oil or steamed and served with a good hoisin sauce or garlic-butter. In writing this I am making myself hungry for collard tops. I can hardly wait for spring!

Stir-Fried Carrots *and* Collard Tops

SERVES 3

If you don't do a lot of stir-frying already, think of this recipe as a model. The method works for most vegetables, though some need braising and others don't. I use unrefined peanut oil for stir-frying, because it is both deliciously fragrant and tolerant of high heat, but you can use refined vegetable oil instead. The soy sauce can be Japanese or Chinese; the fish sauce Thai, Vietnamese, or Korean. Fermented black beans are a dried food available in some Chinese markets; if you can't find them, you can leave them out or use chile-black bean sauce from a jar or something similar, perhaps made with another sort of bean. Sweet chile-garlic sauce comes from Thailand or Vietnam in a tall bottle and is often labeled as sauce for spring rolls or chicken. I often substitute either a homemade version made with fruit juice or a chile-free fruit syrup or fruit molasses. Use only firm or extra-firm tofu; softer tofu can't be stir-fried (though you can firm it somewhat by pressing it between plates lined with paper towels). Before you begin cooking, gather all the ingredients and place them next to the stove along with your serving dish and the lid of the wok.

To "roll-cut" the carrots, slice them diagonally, making one-quarter turns between cuts.

2 tablespoons fermented black beans

Boiling water

Unrefined peanut oil

4 ounces (113 g) green onions, sliced diagonally about ³⁄₁₆ in. (4.8 mm) wide

4 quarter-size slices fresh ginger, minced

3 garlic cloves, minced

8 ounces (227 g) collard or kale tops

Sake or other rice wine

4 ounces (113 g) carrots, roll-cut

1 pound (454 g) firm tofu, cubed

2 tablespoons soy sauce

1 teaspoon fish sauce

2 teaspoons sweet chile-garlic sauce

1 teaspoon roasted sesame oil

Cooked brown or white rice, for serving

1. Put the fermented black beans into a small bowl, and pour over them just enough boiling water to cover them. Let them stand for 15 to 30 minutes.

2. Heat a wok over high heat. Pour in a little oil, and swirl it around. Add the green onions, and stir-fry them very briefly. Add the garlic and ginger, and toss. As soon as you smell the garlic, scrape the ingredients into the serving dish.

3. Return the wok to high heat, pouring in a little more oil if needed, and add the collard or kale tops. Stir-fry them briefly, until their color intensifies a bit and they turn shiny. Add a glug of rice wine, reduce the heat, and put the lid on the wok. Let the collard or kale tops simmer briefly, until they are just tender. Scrape them into the serving dish.

4. Return the wok to the high heat, pouring in a little more oil if needed, and add the carrots. Stir-fry them briefly, until their color intensifies a bit and they turn shiny. Add a glug of rice wine, reduce the heat, and put the lid on the wok. Let the carrots simmer until they are just tender, about 3 minutes. Scrape them into the serving dish.

5. Return the wok to the high heat, pour in a little oil, and swirl it around. Add the tofu. Turn it occasionally and gently, until it is heated through. Reduce the heat to medium, and pour the soy sauce onto the side of the pan to scorch it a bit as it runs to the bottom. Add the black beans and their soaking liquid. Add the fish sauce and sweet chile-garlic sauce. Turn the tofu gently, and let it simmer in the sauce for 1 to 2 minutes. Raise the heat to high, add the vegetables from the serving dish, and toss gently. Turn off the heat, pour the sesame oil over the mixture, and put the lid on the wok. Let the ingredients rest together for about 30 seconds, and then scrape them into the serving dish.

6. Serve immediately, with rice.

Artichokes, Succulent Thistle Buds

*A*fter the city of Lebanon created its first community garden, on an empty lot in the poorest part of town, I signed up for a plot—about 12 by 20 ft. (3.7 by 6 m), full of rocks and broken glass and other debris, but bearing rich clay soil. I was longing for plants I had no room for in the backyard, such as corn, and I looked forward to meeting the other gardeners and sharing plants and advice.

That spring, another gardener brought a flat of artichoke seedlings that a friend had raised. She set one plant in her plot and left the rest of the little pots sitting on the patio in the center of our circle of plots, for anyone to take. No one did. The pots sat there for a day, and then another day. I knew the seedlings wouldn't survive much longer without care, but I didn't need more artichoke plants myself. I asked the garden coordinator if I might plant them in a community plot that so far bore only a few tufts of coneflower. She had no objection, and so I dug holes in the cold, compacted clay, shoveled in some compost, hacked a bit at the ground, and set the artichoke plants, about eight in all.

They required nothing but a little water now and then. Only three or four plants produced buds the first year—the buds are the part that you eat—but this meant that two to three dozen beautiful green artichokes were soon looking for homes. I urged the other gardeners to take some. Mostly I was ignored. I pressed artichokes into reluctant arms. I learned that my fellow gardeners had never eaten artichokes before. I had to explain how to cook them.

This didn't surprise me. Years before I'd lined my driveway with artichoke plants, and passersby regularly asked me what the big, silvery thistles were. I set out a sign to tell them. Every year, the plants produce hundreds of buds. No one has ever stolen any, even though our town has so much poverty that cans and bottles intended for recycling are routinely taken for the dime each will bring. None of the neighbors have suggested they might like to taste one of the big buds. To the people of my town, the artichokes are just interesting-looking plants. Those more in the know wonder why I cut off the buds instead of letting them open into big purple flowers.

I grow artichokes for eating, not for big purple flowers. I grew up eating artichokes. But I am not an Oregon native. I grew up in California, where artichoke farming is an industry and nearly everybody eats artichokes. This is a legacy of the state's Spanish, French, and, most of all, Italian history.

The Spanish probably grew artichokes in the gardens of the California missions. But it was the great wave of Italian immigration in the 1890s that made artichokes a regular part of the California diet. Italians planted artichokes along the coast of the San Francisco Peninsula, especially around Half Moon Bay, where the plants thrived in the cool fog. By 1906, two thousand acres were in production. Then the farmers realized how much more money they could make by selling to fellow Italians in New York, New Jersey, Pennsylvania, Connecticut, and Massachusetts; an artichoke that sold for a nickel in San Francisco would go for a dollar in the East. The farmers formed a marketing organization to ship artichokes to the East Coast, where pushcart and market vendors sold them to Italian immigrants.

And then the mob got involved. A New York gangster named Terranova was determined to corner the artichoke market. He sent his henchman to beat up any distributor who wouldn't sell all his artichokes to Terranova at a painfully low price. Then he sent other mobsters to California. In the "artichoke wars" of 1930, the gangsters intimidated farmers into selling to them direct and cheap, attacked fields of the noncompliant with machetes, highjacked trucks, seized rail cargo, and cracked heads. They often packed illegal liquor into shipping crates along with artichokes. Competing racketeers tried to steal crates, and gun battles broke out. Finally, in 1935, the mayor of New York, Fiorello La Guardia, reacted to the mayhem on both coasts by banning the sale and possession of artichokes in New York. The news spurred non-Italians to try artichokes, and demand for the thistle buds soared. Some of the criminals were prosecuted, and the ban was lifted.

For Italian immigrants, California artichokes, however expensive, were a necessity. For other Northeasterners, they became a luxury vegetable. Elsewhere, artichokes remained mostly unknown. Although they had once been a popular crop in Louisiana, and although Thomas Jefferson grew them at Monticello, for most Americans they never became part of the food culture.

In 1922, commercial artichoke production began well south of the Peninsula, in the lower Salinas River Valley, around Castroville. Today three-quarters of California artichokes are grown in the Castroville area, and California supplies all the artichokes for the national market.

Californians don't just *eat* artichokes. Many grow them in their home gardens, too. The plants are, after all, little trouble to grow. Seeds of the traditional California variety, 'Green Globe', are easy to come by. Plants grown from these seeds may not turn out entirely uniform; the buds may be round or elongated, the bracts may be tightly closed on top or slightly open, and the bracts may or may not bear prominent spines. For these reasons, Castroville farmers always propagate their plants by division. For home gardeners, though, the differences are minor and unimportant.

This is how you grow artichokes: You plant seeds in late winter—here in the Pacific Northwest, in late February or March. I recommend 4 in. (10 cm) pots, in a greenhouse or under grow lights. The seeds may take as long as three weeks to germinate. Prepare a bed of well-drained soil enriched with compost, and set out the young plants, 3 to 5 ft. (1 to 1.5 m) apart, in mid-spring. If they are to set buds the first year, they need to "vernalize"—that is, to chill—for four to five weeks with nighttime temperatures no higher than 50°F (10°C). If frost threatens during this period, protect the plants.

Once they are established, the plants need little care. They are impressively drought resistant. I water my plants only two or three times through the summer.

The harvest continues so long that you may get tired of eating artichokes. First-year plants will begin producing buds in early summer; older plants will produce continuously through the spring and into the summer and may bear a smaller crop in the fall, too. My plants produce good buds continuously through

the spring and early summer, after which the buds become somewhat tough. They are still edible in the heat of summer, but they require longer cooking (more frequent watering might help). Then the bud formation stops, and it restarts only briefly in the fall.

Vernalization may be difficult in regions without a long, cool spring. Gardeners in colder places may prefer to grow artichokes as annuals. These gardeners should look for seeds of cultivars developed in the 1980s by Keith Mayberry, whose artichokes require a vernalization period of only about ten days. His varieties include 'Imperial Star', the purple 'Colorado Star', and 'Tavor' and 'Purple Tavor'. In warmer areas, these can all be grown as perennials.

Dozens of other artichoke varieties have been developed. Rusty Jordan, of Big Heart Seed, in California, has bred an assortment of hybrid cultivars for annual planting, but they are generally unavailable to home gardeners. Most other varieties are Italian; some are French. They vary in plant height, hardiness, earliness, and bud size, shape, and color. Many have beautiful red-purple buds. Unfortunately, seeds of the European cultivars are scarce, and so is information about them. But I encourage you to try them if you can get seeds and if you have the patience to experiment.

The hardest part about growing artichokes is knowing when to harvest the buds. Size isn't a good determinant, since buds grow bigger on central stalks and smaller on side stalks. It's important to cut the buds while they feel firm and before the bracts have opened. But even if you follow this rule, a bud at harvest may have developed a "choke," the fluffy fiber that makes up the upper part of the seed pod and that would become the purple flower if you waited long enough. This is the stage at which artichokes are sold in supermarkets. These artichokes are usable, if you either dig out the choke or peel away the bracts, one by one, and then spoon the choke away from the meaty bottom. But it's better to harvest the buds when they are less mature, before the chokes develop. In other words, it's wise to err on the side of earliness.

It's also wise to cut the buds with 3 to 4 in. (7.5 to 10 cm) of stem, because the upper stem is tender and tasty. The cut end will blacken soon after cutting, but you can simply trim off a bit before cooking.

When your artichoke plants have finished producing, they will begin to turn dry and brown. Cut them to the ground, mulch them well, and wait for the tops to come back. Mine send up new shoots in fall, after the rains begin,

and in a mild winter they just keep growing. Extended below-freezing weather will knock them back, but they re-emerge when the temperatures begin to rise.

After some years—say, five to ten—you should divide the plants, or the buds will get progressively smaller.

Preparing artichokes for the table can be very simple. When I was a child, my mother simply boiled them whole and served them with mayonnaise. We'd peel off the bracts one at a time, dip them in the mayonnaise, and then scrape off the tender flesh at the base of the bract with our teeth. When we finished with the bracts we'd remove the choke, dip the bottom in the mayonnaise, and eat it whole.

As a grown-up I have refined this dish only slightly. I stand my artichokes snugly together in a pot and add about an inch of water, so that they will steam more than boil. I add a clove of garlic, salt, and a splash of olive oil before I cook them. I serve them with homemade aioli. Because I usually harvest my artichokes young, there are seldom chokes to remove, and we eat the hearts of the artichokes whole.

Italians and other Europeans use a basic trimming technique that readies artichokes for many other uses. You bend back the outer petals of a young artichoke and tear them off at the base. Keep pulling off the petals until you're holding a cone that is yellow in its bottom half and light green at the top. Cut off the top of the cone, removing the tough green portion. The petals of the finished heart should be so tightly wrapped that they are difficult to tear away. Trim away any green bits remaining at the base of the artichoke. Trim off as much of the stem as you like; you might want to use the stems separately. To keep your artichoke hearts from browning as you work, rub them with lemon juice.

Now you have fully edible, delicious artichoke nuggets that can be used in any number of dishes. After boiling or steaming them you might simply serve them with garlic butter, perhaps with lemon juice added. You might pickle them in vinegar, or you might halve the artichokes and finish them on a grill. You might roast your artichokes, in embers or in an oven, drenched in olive oil and covered in foil. You might deep-fry them and serve them with a tahini sauce, or quarter them and cook them in a stew of spring vegetables or add them to a pasta sauce of tomato and wine and clams. You might sauté them, quartered, in olive oil with garlic, and then add chunks of potatoes and braise

the vegetables together. If you pick your artichokes very young, you might slice them thin and serve them raw, dressed with olive oil and lemon juice.

Do beware in serving artichokes that, for most people, they make liquids taste strangely sweet. A compound called cynarin in artichokes temporarily blocks the sweet taste receptors. When the liquid washes away the cynarin, the sweet receptors misinterpret the change as a stimulus, and the liquid tastes sweet. This can be amusing when you're drinking water but annoying when you're drinking an expensive wine. For this reason, sommeliers struggle over the question of what wines to serve with artichokes. Some recommend bubbly wines, others very acidic wines. You might just eat your artichokes as a first course and save the wine for a second course.

In the community garden, the artichoke plants that hadn't budded in the first year shot up and began producing early in the second year. The other plants soon followed. To my surprise, the buds, when they reached full size, began disappearing. Apparently, the gardeners on whom I'd pressed artichokes and preparation advice the year before were now quietly harvesting the buds themselves. I didn't have to take any home. That's because everybody—everybody who tries them—loves artichokes.

Pickled Artichoke Hearts

MAKES 8 CUPS (1.9 L)

Commercially packed marinated artichoke hearts can be delicious, but making your own is cheap and easy, if you have your own artichoke plants. Here I save on olive oil by leaving it out of the jar and just drizzling some over the artichoke hearts at serving time.

About 1 gallon small, firm artichokes

1 lemon, halved

2 thyme sprigs

2 oregano sprigs

1 ½ cups (355 mL) white wine vinegar (at least 5 percent)

2 ½ cups (591 mL) water

½ teaspoon whole black peppercorns, crushed

½ teaspoon hot pepper flakes

4 garlic cloves, sliced

2 tablespoons pickling salt

1 teaspoon sugar

Olive oil

1. Pull the outer leaves off each artichoke, until the yellowish heart is exposed around the stem. With a sharp knife, cut about ½ in. (1.25 cm) off the top of the artichoke. Stand the artichoke upside-down, and slice downward and slightly inward to trim off the dark portions of the remaining leaves. Be unsparing, so you end up with only the tender, yellow-green core. As you work, rub each trimmed artichoke with a lemon half.

2. In a saucepan, bring to a boil enough water to cover the artichoke hearts. Squeeze the lemon halves into the water. Add the artichoke hearts and cook until they are tender, 15 to 20 minutes.

3. Drain the artichoke hearts well. Pack them into a 2-quart jar, and tuck in the herb sprigs along the inside of the jar.

4. Combine the vinegar, water, peppercorns, pepper flakes, pickling salt, and sugar in a saucepan. Cover the pan and bring the mixture to a boil. Pour the hot liquid over the artichokes and close the jar.

5. Store the jar in the refrigerator for at least a week before eating the artichokes. Serve them drizzled with olive oil.

6. Refrigerated, the artichokes should keep well for months.

Leaves
of the Vine

You can't grow grapes in the Willamette Valley without producing an astounding amount of leafy vine. Would-be wine growers look for hillsides and thinner soils for planting, so that the vines don't overwhelm the fruit, shading it from the sunshine that is essential for ripening. Even on poorer land farmers must thin the leaves in summer if they want to produce wine that's fit to drink. On the lowlands, the soils are so rich and the water table usually so high that irrigation is a bad idea after the first year or two. Even without irrigation, you can't have your grapes without a lot of excess foliage.

The situation is more astonishing still with table grapes. Most of the table grape varieties suitable for growing beyond the drier parts of California and the Mediterranean region are not *Vitis vinifera*, the Eurasian wine grape, but American species or American-European hybrids. Americans once thought themselves more vigorous than their European cousins. In the case of grapes, this extra vigor is a fact.

When you witness the gusto with which sheep tear the leaves from grape-vines extending over a pasture fence—or when you see the sheep escape from the pasture and run straight for the grape trellis—you must surmise that the leaves are very good food. They are, indeed; in particular, they are full of vitamin A. They also provide substantial quantities of vitamin K, magnesium, calcium, iron, and zinc. Although people aren't ruminants, we have been eating grape leaves for centuries, perhaps for thousands of years. We have used the leaves for their tannins in pickling, to help keep vegetables firm, and in salads. Above all, we have used the leaves for dolma, the Turkish name for something stuffed, a food with an edible wrapper. Turks and people throughout the former Ottoman Empire love stuffed foods—cabbage leaves, peppers, eggplants, cucumbers, onions, quinces, and especially, in summer, grape leaves. Stuffed grape leaves are popular over such a broad area that they have many names—*sarma, dolmeh, dolmades, tolma, yebra, mahshi,* and more.

Long before I'd covered three trellises on the farm with table grapevines, I was picking the leaves to line my pickle crocks. Eventually I decided that the sheep would have to share more of the plentiful leaves, because I was going to make grape-leaf dolmas. Dolmas are not a typical food of Oregon. But Oregonians have grown quite proud of their grapes, as evidenced by the price of Oregon wines. Why shouldn't we be cooking with grape leaves?

I wouldn't eat grape leaves from our home wine vineyard. To grow wine grapes in western Oregon, you must spray them with fungicides. Sulfur may wash off, but other chemicals may not. Besides, the leaves of most wine varieties, even when clean, are far from ideal, as they can be small, tough, wrinkled, and deeply lobed. For dolmas, you want fairly big, flat, tender, shallowly lobed leaves.

Beyond any wine vineyard are many possible sources of suitable grape leaves for dolmas. My most productive table grape, in terms of fruit and leaves both, has been 'Canadice'. 'Canadice' leaves are excellent for wrapping. Here in town I also have a 'Himrod' vine, and its leaves are equally big, flat, and tender. For people in hotter, drier places, 'Thompson Seedless', a *vinifera* variety, is the leaf of choice. Some people make dolmas with leaves of wild grapevines and claim success, although the suitability of these leaves depends on the particular species. There are many grape species in North America, and none of them have toxic leaves, unless they are sprayed with poisons. But some may be too tough or tannic for dolmas. The leaves of *Vitis labrusca*, or fox grapes, from eastern North America, have whitish, felty undersides. Maybe these leaves are usable anyway; I don't know. I've grown some *vinifera-labrusca* hybrids that have these felted leaves, and I've avoided picking them for dolmas.

If you're considering a particular grapevine for dolmas, I suggest examining the leaves, making sure that they are unsprayed, and then tasting them. They should have a mild but tangy flavor.

Once you've found a good vine, keep in mind that not all the leaves are equally suitable. You'll notice that the last leaves on a vine are small, yellow-green, and very tender. Ignore the last three leaves, and pick the three before them. They should be shiny and tender, but bigger. Farther back on the vine you'll see dull, dark leaves. These would be too tough, and perhaps too big as well, for modest-size dolmas. Let the sheep have them.

In case you don't get around to making your dolmas immediately, you can keep the leaves in a plastic bag in the refrigerator for several days.

Here in western Oregon, grapevines keep growing and producing new, tender leaves until fall. This means I have about four months to make dolmas from grape leaves before moving on to other stuffed foods, like cabbage. So I seldom bother to preserve grape leaves for winter.

Many people do preserve grape leaves, however, in various ways. You can blanch the leaves in salted water and then freeze them; some people roll and tie stacks of leaves and blanch the whole stacks at once. Or, after blanching, you can put them up in jars. Just pack them in rolls into sterilized canning jars, cover the leaves with lemon juice and hot water in a 1:4 ratio, or with hot water acidified with citric acid (1 teaspoon citric acid for 2 ½ cups, or 591 mL, water), and give the jars a fifteen-minute boiling-water bath. Or you can ferment your grape leaves, in the same way you ferment cucumbers, for one to two weeks. Store the fermented leaves in the refrigerator, or boil the brine, pour it over the leaves in a canning jar, and give the jar a fifteen-minute boiling-water bath.

If you're adding grape leaves to your pickle crock to help keep your pickles firm, choose leaves that are suitable for dolmas. Later you can remove the leaves, rinse them, and fill them without blanching them first. They will make especially flavorful dolmas.

Dolmas *with* Mint *and* Pine Nuts

MAKES 40 TO 50 DOLMAS

Because I'm not fond of ground meat, this is a meatless recipe. The pine nuts provide protein, richness, and textural contrast. They are, of course, very expensive, so I often use chopped roasted hazelnuts in their place. Other nuts might also work well in this recipe. Instead of garlic chives, you can use regular chives, Egyptian walking onions, or other green onions (see "Petite, Perpetual Garlic Chives," and "The Onion That Walks").

1 cup (185 g) medium-grain rice

40 to 50 fresh, tender, medium-size grape leaves

½ cup (118 mL) chopped garlic chives

1 cup (235 mL) minced spearmint

1 teaspoon fine salt

½ cup (71 g) pine nuts

3 tablespoons lemon juice

¼ cup (60 mL) olive oil

1. Put the rice in a bowl and pour over boiling water to cover the rice well. Let the rice soak for 30 minutes.

2. With kitchen shears, trim the stems off the grape leaves.

3. In a large saucepan, bring about 3 in. (7.5 cm) of water to a simmer. Immerse the grape leaves, a few at a time, pressing them under the water. When the leaves are limp and olive green, after 10 to 20 seconds, transfer them to a colander or towel to drain.

4. When the rice has finished soaking, rinse it in cold water, and drain well. In a bowl, combine the rice with the garlic chives, mint, salt, pine nuts, lemon juice, and olive oil.

5. Line the bottom and sides of a medium saucepan with about six of the grape leaves (use any that are torn or oversize). Prop the pan with a rolled towel to hold it at an angle, so you can keep the dolmas upright as you add them to the pan.

6. One at a time, lay the grape leaves flat, dull-side up, with the stem end closest to your body. Place a heaping teaspoonful of the rice mixture (or a little more, if the leaf is large) near the stem end and fold the two lower parts of the leaf over the mixture. Fold in the sides of the leaf, and roll it up, folding in the sides once more if they will protrude otherwise. Place the rolled leaves vertically in the pan until the pan is full and you've used all the filling.

7. Lay the remaining grape leaves on top of the dolmas to keep them in place. Add about 1 in. (2.5 cm) boiling water to the pan. Cover the pan and simmer the dolmas for about 40 minutes. Remove the pan from the heat and remove the lid.

8. When the dolmas are cool enough to handle, transfer them to a serving dish. Serve them hot, warm, or cool.

9. If you refrigerate some of the dolmas for later use, cover them with their cooking liquid so the rice doesn't get hard.

Petite, Perpetual Garlic Chives

*T*his sweet, mild-flavored onion plant gives and gives and gives, year after year and nearly year-round, while remaining tidily in its place.

East Asians know the value of this plant. Garlic chives (so-called for their light garlic flavor) are also known as Chinese chives or Chinese leeks, and rightly so. They are native to Shanxi, in northern China, and the Chinese have been eating them for three thousand years.

In recent centuries garlic chives have been making their way around the world. They are beloved by cooks in Japan, Korea, Southeast Asia, northern India, and central Asia. The USDA reports that they grow wild in Ohio, Wisconsin, Iowa, and Nebraska, and in parts of Australia and Europe they are considered invasive. I wonder whether Midwesterners, Australians, and Europeans take advantage of this bounty, or whether they scorn these little onions as too common. If most aren't using garlic chives yet, I hope they will begin.

Garlic chives have flat leaves, like leeks. The plants grow only ¼ in. (0.5 cm) wide and 8 to 18 in. (20 to 46 cm) high. As young garlic chives develop, they form rhizomes, through which the plants spread into clumps (this is the reason for

the botanical name, *Allium tuberosum*, although the plants don't form tubers). The clumps grow, over several years, to about 12 in. (30 cm) in diameter. In late summer, hollow flower stalks rise over the clumps. If the stalks are picked before the buds open, they are tender enough to eat but sturdy enough to use as a vegetable in a stir-fry. In early fall the little white flowers open, in umbels. Then the plants prove their worth to ornamental gardeners, who admire the flowering clumps along a garden path, and especially to beekeepers, whose charges relish the late-season forage.

Although garlic chives are very hardy, the plants die back in winter with a hard frost. But they return in early spring; usually I can begin cutting them in March. In warmer climates, they can be harvested year-round.

After you cut them, they grow right back.

Asian breeders have developed various cultivars of garlic chives. Some cultivars are favored for their leaves, others for their tender flower stalks. Some are preferred for blanching, to produce tender yellow leaves that are used in noodle and seafood dishes. But in the United States in general you are likely to find the plant, or the seeds, labeled simply "garlic chives" or "Chinese chives."

Garlic chive seeds can be started in flats or in the ground. If you start them in a flat, you might transplant several or a dozen together to get a clump established faster. One clump may be enough for your household, but if you really like garlic chives you may want several clumps, so that you don't exhaust any of the plants by harvesting too often.

If you have little garden space or want your garlic chives close to the kitchen door, you might plant them in a pot. With their slow growth and pretty flowers, they make excellent container plants.

Garlic chives like full sun and rich, well-drained soil, but they aren't fussy. They will tolerate partial shade, and they need only occasional irrigation. Let the soil dry out between waterings.

Harvest garlic chives by cutting them close to the ground. You'll see that, like a scallion, each has a white lower section and a green upper one. You might want to separate the two and cook the bottom sections separately and longer, if you cook them at all. The flavor of garlic chives is so mild that they—even the white sections—are easy to eat raw.

At some point you might want to try blanching a clump of garlic chives. You can do this simply by covering the clump with a pot, just after harvest of the green chives. But do this no more than once a season, because it weakens the plant.

When the plant sends up flower stalks, in late summer, you don't have to stop harvesting. Use the flower stalks separately—they will need to be cooked—and use the green leaves as before. You might want to add the closed buds to salads or pickle them. When the buds open, you may prefer to leave the blossoms to the honeybees, though open garlic chive flowers are also edible and have a strong oniony flavor. Some Chinese pound and ferment them into a condiment.

Soon the plants produce little black seeds. You can save them for planting or let them fall to the ground. If you leave them alone, some will grow into baby plants that you can share or plant elsewhere. If you don't want your plants reproducing on their own, just clip off the tops before the seeds mature. You can use the clipped seed heads in dried flower arrangements.

Unless you live in a warm climate, the plants will go dormant over the winter. You might cover a clump with a cloche to extend the harvest or bring a potted clump indoors. In the spring, you can give your clumps a boost by spreading a little compost around them. After a few years, your clumps may begin to weaken. Dig them, divide them, and reset the smaller clumps.

Now, what will you do with all your garlic chives? You can chop them and add them to miso soup or yogurt soup. You might use them to garnish cold peanut noodles, stir-fried tofu, or practically any other dish. You might slice them into pieces, say, 1 to 1½ in. (2.5 to 4 cm), and incorporate them in place of scallions in cabbage kimchi. You might combine them with ground meat in Chinese dumplings. You might sauté two or three handfuls and combine them with potatoes in a salad. And you might use garlic chives generously, as Chinese people often do, in scrambled eggs.

Chinese-Style Scrambled Eggs *with* Garlic Chives

The cornstarch in this recipe is said to make the eggs fluffier, but I think it makes them more solid and layered. If you prefer you can leave out the cornstarch, and the same goes for the rice wine and sugar. No matter how you prepare your scrambled eggs, in fact, garlic chives are a lovely addition.

5 large eggs

2 pinches of sugar

¼ teaspoon salt, or more, to taste

1 teaspoon rice wine (preferably Shaoxing, for a richer flavor)

½ teaspoon roasted sesame oil

1 teaspoon cornstarch mixed with 1 tablespoon water

1 to 1 ½ cups (50 to 75 g) chopped garlic chives

1 tablespoon peanut oil or other vegetable oil

1. Crack the eggs into a bowl, and beat well. Add the sugar, salt, rice wine, sesame oil, and cornstarch slurry, and beat again. Stir in the garlic chives.

2. Heat a wok or frying pan over medium-high heat. When it is quite hot, reduce the heat to medium-low. Add the peanut oil, and swirl the pan to distribute the oil over the surface. Pour in the egg mixture. As the mixture begins to set, turn it gently. As soon as the eggs are fully cooked, transfer them to a serving dish. Serve immediately.

103

Green Garbanzos

I first found them about a decade ago in a Salem, Oregon, super-market: small yellow-green pods, each cradling one or, usually, two round green seeds. Fresh garbanzos! I shelled them like peas and boiled them for about five minutes before tossing them into a salad. Cooked, they had a flavor that was pea-like, though less sweet, and a firm texture with none of the mealiness of dried garbanzos. They were very much like edamame—green soybeans—but tastier. My dinner guests startled at the cooked garbanzos' bright yellow-green color.

An ancient food of the Mediterranean region, southern Asia, and North Africa, garbanzos, or chickpeas, need a long, rather cool growing season in well-drained soil. So where had these pods come from, in early April? I guessed southern California, and a little sleuthing around the Internet reinforced my suspicion. A company called Califresh was established near Fresno in 2002 specifically to produce green garbanzos, after the founders saw Mexican immigrants selling uprooted plants, their green pods dangling, along the roadsides of southern California. Green garbanzos had long been a popular snack in Mexico, and Mexican immigrant communities were a ready market. Soon Califresh had expanded production to several Californian and Mexican growing areas so the company could supply the fresh market year-round. And the market is wherever a lot of Mexicans have settled—as they have, in recent years, in and around Salem, Oregon.

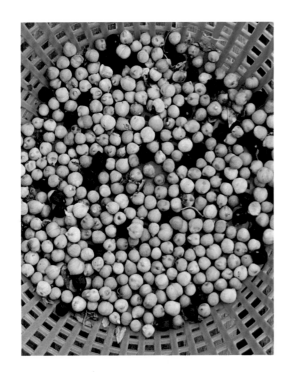

And how do Mexicans eat green garbanzos? Usually boiled in the pod, I learned, and then popped straight from the pod into the mouth, just as the Japanese eat edamame. I wondered if Japanese immigrants could have introduced Mexicans to the idea of snacking on boiled pod beans. Many Japanese migrated to Mexico after the two countries signed a formal agreement over trade and immigration in 1888. Most took jobs in the mines, on sugar plantations, and on railroads. In 1912, *Metropolitan Magazine* described a new Japanese settlement of fishermen, divers, boatbuilders, and farmers on Manzanillo Bay, on the west coast of Mexico. The proprietors had a concession to use 800 miles (1,287 km) of shore, and all the rivers, lakes, and lagoons in the area, from Manzanillo south to Salina Cruz, in Oaxaca. Eight thousand Japanese had already arrived. The farmers' job was to grow food for the others.

When World War II began, the U.S. government, fearing a Japanese invasion, pressed Mexico to move its Japanese population inland to Mexico City and Guadalajara. Some of the Manzanillo Japanese undoubtably ended up in Guadalajara, which is only 180 miles (290 km) from Manzanilla Bay. Guadalajara is the capital of the state of Jalisco, and Jalisco produces 75 percent of Mexico's forage garbanzos—that is, garbanzos for pigs and cows.

Apparently not all those garbanzos go to livestock. Jalisco is the place best known for *guasanas*—that is, green garbanzos, which are also known in Mexico as *garbanzas* and *garbanzos verdes*. They are boiled in salted water, drained, and served in the pod. Or they are prepared in a way that seems more in keeping with indigenous culinary traditions: They are toasted in their pods on a comal or in a skillet until the pods are golden brown. Sometimes they are steamed first, and then toasted until dry. Whatever the method, street vendors sell them in cones folded from newspaper.

I had never grown garbanzos, for either fresh or dried use. Now I wanted to do it, just for the treat of my own green garbanzos. And in growing my own I could try red, black, and brown garbanzos, from among the dozen or more varieties listed by Seed Savers Exchange. I wondered if I could really manage to grow them, though, with my heavy soil and short growing season.

Garbanzos can indeed be grown in cooler places. Thanks in part to the current craze for hummus, they are now a major commercial crop in eastern Washington, western Idaho, and Montana, and farmers also grow them in North Dakota, South Dakota, and eastern Oregon. For a time even a few farmers here in the Willamette Valley produced them. Garbanzos proved an iffy crop for commercial farmers in this rainy land, but home gardeners here and elsewhere can do well with them.

Garbanzos are usually planted in early spring, because the plants need at least three months to produce filled pods and longer for the pods to dry. Our wet soils of spring and cold rains of autumn can be problematic, but producing green garbanzos is much easier than producing dry ones.

A friend had already given me some seeds of 'Hannan Popbean', a brown-to black-seeded chickpea selected by Carol Deppe, a Corvallis plant breeder. Carol calls this bean a popbean not because the pods make a little popping noise as you press them open (sometimes they do) but because she pops the dried seeds like corn, by parching them in a hot, dry pan until they swell and break open. Not all garbanzo varieties will pop this way.

Garbanzo varieties are classed with terminology originating in India. Colored beans like Carol's are classed as Desi, a Hindi word for "local." Big, cream-colored, round Kabouli garbanzos, once thought to have come from Afghanistan, were introduced to India much later. Desi beans tend to be small and angular, and they are usually grown in hotter areas. Kabouli garbanzos would probably have been a better choice for me, since I wasn't interested in parching the beans; I wanted to use them green. But I didn't know anything about garbanzo varieties at the time, and, after all, Carol's growing conditions were much the same as mine.

Although Carol grows her popbeans in early spring, without irrigation, I planted mine on the farm in late May, along with soybeans, runner beans, long beans, and bush snap-beans (*Phaseolus vulgaris*). A couple of weeks after the initial planting I had to fill big gaps in the other bean rows, but to my surprise every one of the garbanzos germinated. Not long after, I was surprised again, this time by the ferny garbanzo foliage, which looks much like vetch and nothing like other bean leaves. The third surprise from my garbanzo row was the best one: Deer don't bother these plants. I learned why they don't

when I ate my first green garbanzo, just two months after planting, and tasted something sharply sour on my fingers. I touched my tongue to a bean pod and understood: The plant defends itself from grazing by seasoning its pods and foliage with acids—mostly malic, a little oxalic. Brilliant! In India farmers lay cloths over their garbanzo plants in the evening and then squeeze the cloths in the morning to extract the acids.

So I let go of my fears about all the special requirements for growing garbanzos. I didn't have a long growing season. I didn't have sandy soil (though I do now, since moving to town). I didn't add nitrogen-fixing bacteria to the soil. But I didn't need any of these things. Garbanzos seemed to be an excellent crop for my garden. They were certainly easier to grow than edamame.

Carol's 'Hannan Popbean' served well for green garbanzos. The seeds, I found, stayed green until they began drying. In harvesting, I chose pods that were well filled but still green for boiling; the ones that had turned yellow-brown I saved for drying.

Here are guidelines for growing your own garbanzos: Plant them when the soil has warmed to 45°F (7°C), as early as March but no later than early May (they can tolerate spring frosts). If you live in a very cold place, you might start your garbanzos indoors—in biodegradable pots, because they don't like their roots disturbed. For better yields, consider inoculating the seeds with *Rhizobium* bacteria (though I have not). Irrigation probably isn't necessary. Watch out for tobacco budworms, which will eat a hole in each pod and devour the green seeds inside. If you see these holes, pick off the worms in the evenings. Harvest the green pods one at a time or pull whole plants if most of the pods are ready. Either way, wear gloves if the acid irritates your skin. If you prefer to harvest the pods dry, wait until they have turned brown, and then pull the plants. Lay them in a dry place, and bring them indoors before the rains start, or the beans will get moldy. Shell the dried seeds by hand or by dancing on the pods.

Boiled *and* Toasted Green Garbanzos

SERVES 2

This is the most complex of the three cooking methods here, but it has three advantages: The garbanzos absorb some salt during boiling, the toasting time is shortened, and the toasted pods turn out dry, not soggy. You can do the boiling ahead of time so that just before serving you need only to toast the garbanzos.

6 cups (1.4 L) water

1 tablespoon salt

2 teaspoons oil (optional)

8 ounces (227 g) green garbanzos, in their pods

1. Put the water and salt in a pot, and bring the water to a boil. Add the garbanzos, and cook them for 4 minutes, stirring occasionally.

2. Drain the pods in a broad, flat-bottomed colander. Heat a large skillet or comal over high heat. If you are using a cast-iron skillet, coat it with the oil, so the steaming garbanzos don't cause the skillet to rust. Add the garbanzos, and toast them, turning them often, until they have lightly browned in spots, about 10 minutes. Serve them hot.

Boiled Green Garbanzos

SERVES 2

This is the simplest and quickest way to prepare green garbanzos. Served in the pod, they are very similar to green soybeans prepared the same way, but to me green garbanzos are much tastier.

6 cups (1.4 L) water

Salt

8 ounces (227 g) green garbanzos, in their pods

1. Put the water and at least 1 tablespoon of salt in a pot, and bring the water to a boil. Add the garbanzos, and cook them for about 5 minutes, stirring occasionally. Small-seeded garbanzos need a little less cooking time.

2. Drain the pods in a broad, flat-bottomed colander. Sprinkle them with more salt, and serve them immediately.

Toasted Green Garbanzos

SERVES 2

Salting these is ineffective; salt doesn't stick to dry pods as it does to wet ones. The garbanzos turn out delicious anyway.

8 ounces (227 g) green garbanzos, in their pods

Heat a large frying pan (or a comal, if you have one) over medium heat. Add the garbanzos. Toast them, turning often, until they are golden brown, about 20 minutes. Serve them hot.

Magenta-Leafed Orach

One of the first plants to sprout in my vegetable garden each spring—randomly among the beds and between them in the gravel—is orach, its little red leaves bright against the soil and stones. In time it begins to go to seed, sending up a stalk at least 3 ft. (1 m) tall that bears opposite pairs of 2 to 3 in. (5 to 7.5 cm) heart-shaped leaves. Sometimes I pinch back the top of each plant to encourage it to bush out, but I often don't bother. Orach's harvest season is long regardless, and the small leaves at the top of the plant are never bitter or tough. They are perfect for adding whole to green salads.

Orach—pronounced "OR-rich"—is *Atriplex hortensis*, an herb in the amaranth family that comes in green, red, purple, and "white," or bright yellow-green. The plant is related to spinach and chard and tastes like both, only much milder, with barely a touch of sourness. Given plenty of water, red orach can grow as tall as 6 ft. (1.8 m), and green orach is reported as growing as much as 10 ft. (3 m) tall.

I've planted orach only once. Although I save seeds of this plant every year, I end up giving them away. For my own garden, I let at least one plant self-sow. The seeds, in their flat, papery husks (pairs of bracts), are carried by the wind among my garden beds. Usually, just the right number manage to sprout. Wherever the plants arise, I welcome the spot of red color, especially when the breeze exposes the leaves' fuchsia undersides. In the past two summers

I've had purple and "white" orach plants, too, without ever planting them. It seems red orach can spontaneously mutate to these other colors.

Although orach isn't native to Europe, it has grown wild there for so long that its history is obscure. Most sources locate its origin as Central Asia. Frank Morton, of Wild Garden Seeds in Philomath, Oregon, traces its ancestry back to Pangea days, when orach, quinoa, and a Mexican herb called huauzontles were one and the same species. In what became South America, the number of chromosomes in the plant doubled, and the world got quinoa. In what became Asia, the chromosomes tripled, and orach arose. Perhaps traveling on sheep's pelts and wool, orach arrived in the Mediterranean area early enough for the ancient Greeks to write about it. They didn't all like it; Pythagoras accused it of causing dropsy, jaundice, pallor, and digestive problems in humans as well as drooping in nearby plants, and Diocles and Dionysius said it caused numerous diseases, including freckles and pimples. But others thought it good medicine—it has been shown to be mildly laxative and diuretic as well as rich in ascorbic acid—and good food, too.

Orach soon made its way north. The French especially took to it; the English name *orach* comes from the French *arroche*. By 1548 orach was growing in England, in gardens and cornfields. John Gerard mentioned two garden varieties in 1597, white and purple, as well as a "lesser"-leafed wild type. But by 1783 the English were mostly growing spinach instead—although in 1886 British dairy women were still using "white" (yellow-green) orach for wrapping butter.

At some point orach made its way to North America. Thomas Jefferson grew it, and added it to his salads, at Monticello. The Massachusetts horticulturalist Fearing Burr, Jr., claimed to know of sixteen varieties grown in the United States—although, he said, orach was becoming rare in American gardens. Spinach, which thrives in humid conditions, was taking its place in the Eastern states.

Two horticultural researchers in the Great Plains region, M. F. Babb and James E. Kraus, took an interest in orach in the late 1930s, when they found green orach growing on the sites of former gardens. Central Europeans, they believed, had brought the plant to the region. The researchers found that orach grew well at elevations as high as 7,300 ft. (2,225 m) and that even in the driest season it would grow to a height of 4 to 6 ft. (1.2 to 1.8 m) without irrigation. Yet at the time, for some reason, no U.S. seedhouses were offering orach seeds.

It's hard to understand why anyone would prefer spinach to orach. Orach, unlike spinach, tolerates cold climates and somewhat alkaline and salty soils.

Spinach dislikes fluctuating temperatures; in my climate it usually rushes to bolt before I can harvest any leaves. Orach, in contrast, produces tender, tasty leaves over weeks or even months and takes its time to go to seed. Whereas spinach needs regular watering, orach thrives with just one or two irrigations per season. Spinach is always green, but orach shares the bright color range of beets. Once harvested, spinach quickly turns to mush, but orach leaves will keep well in the fridge for a week.

Orach also tends to beat out spinach in taste competitions. A French researcher, R. de Noter, wrote in 1921 that orach sold for three times the price of spinach in his country. Babb and Kraus found that their "cooperators" tended to prefer orach, too. Children usually prefer orach, because its flavor is sweeter and milder than that of spinach.

Cooks who find the taste of orach a little too mild sometimes combine orach with garden sorrel.

Orach is good for more than eating as greens, but its other uses have been little explored in this country. The green leaves have been used to color pasta, and the seeds to produce a blue dye. The seeds are also edible, with a protein content of 25 to 30 percent, higher than that of almonds. One of the French names for orach is blé d'Espagne, "wheat of Spain," and de Noter wrote that "the seeds, milled and bolted into flour, make an excellent feed. . . . In Mexico this brown flour is used to make cakes." Orach stems, which are too tough to eat, can be used to make paper. Orach is a survival plant.

Orach is easy to grow. It's wise to sow the seeds generously, because not all of them sprout readily. They come in two types: large (about ⅛ in. or 3.2 mm) and buff-colored, and small and dark (my little ones are green-gray), with a hard coat. The ratio of big to little seeds varies depending on the variety and growing conditions. Whereas the big seeds sprout quickly, the small ones do not. Frank Morton thinks that the small seeds are a kind of insurance for the plant. They may sprout later, when conditions change around the mother plant, or they may be carried off by birds, whose digestive systems may damage the seed coat in a way that makes sprouting easier without destroying the seed.

Babb and Kraus recommend either of two growing methods: Sow the seeds in rows 20 in. (51 cm) apart, harvest all the plants at 4 to 6 in. (10 to 15 cm), and plant more seeds at two-week intervals, or use a wider spacing and thin the plants until they are 3 ft. (1 m) apart, and then harvest from the remaining plants through the rest of the season.

You can use orach leaves, raw or cooked, in any way that you use spinach. I love red orach for its color in salads, and it is even prettier combined with "white" orach. Frank Morton sells orach in several colors, including 'Ruby Gold', which has found popularity among florists (for arrangements, harvest the tops before the seeds form).

A couple of years ago, something different about the weather slowed my orach's advance to seed production, and I began to appreciate the plant more than ever. It formed lettuce-like heads with big leaves, 5 to 6 in. (13 to 15 cm) across. One day, as I considered what to make for dinner, I figured these leaves might be the only big ones I would get; the plants were already beginning to bolt. So, dinner *had* to include orach salad rolls.

I picked eight big orach leaves, trimmed out the lower part of the midribs, and rolled each leaf around bean-thread noodles, pickled threads of carrot, mint leaves, and salad shrimp. This was much easier than making salad rolls with rice-paper wrappers; the leaves proved to be at once sturdy and flexible. For accompaniment, I made a sweet peanut-chile sauce. I didn't check my watch, but I'll bet that Robert and I ate the whole stack of salad rolls in less than three minutes.

Orach Salad Rolls

SERVES 4 AS A STARTER

I use a Vietnamese variety of mint, but spearmint works well too. For garnish, borage blossoms provide an interesting color contrast.

Quick Carrot Pickle

2 tablespoons rice vinegar

1 ½ teaspoons sugar

¼ teaspoon fine salt

1 medium-large carrot (about 2.5 oz or 70 g)

Sweet Peanut-Chile Sauce

1 tablespoon peanut butter

3 tablespoons Thai sweet chile-garlic sauce

1 tablespoon rice vinegar

¼ teaspoon fine salt

Salad Rolls

Two bunches bean-thread noodles

8 large orach leaves

Handful of fresh mint leaves

½ cup (125 g) salad shrimp (cooked and peeled tiny shrimp), thawed

1. **To make the pickle,** stir together the rice vinegar, sugar, and salt in a wide bowl. Cut the carrot into thin sticks by slicing it diagonally and then cutting the slices thin lengthwise. Toss the carrot in the seasoned vinegar. The sticks will quickly lose their stiffness.

2. **To make the sauce,** put the peanut butter in a small serving bowl. With a fork, mix in the sweet chile-garlic sauce. Add the vinegar to loosen the sauce, and then season the sauce with salt.

3. In a large saucepan, heat water to a boil. Cook the bean-thread noodles until they are tender—less than a minute—separating them with chopsticks as they begin to soften. Drain the noodles, and rinse them well with cold water.

4. Cut out about 1 in. (2.5 cm) of the lower, thicker midrib from each orach leaf. Lay the leaves, one at a time, upside-down on your work surface. Top each leaf with a portion of the noodles, carrot, mint, and shrimp, and roll the leaf from the base to the tip. Place the roll seam-side down on a plate. Repeat with the remaining orach leaves and fillings.

The *The* Singular Makah Ozette Potato

The first time I grew 'Makah Ozette' potatoes, I planted a single tuber in my city garden. The plant that grew yielded nearly thirteen pounds of tubers.

Until recently grown only by the Makah tribe of Washington's Olympic Peninsula, the pale-skinned 'Makah Ozette' is called a fingerling for its elongated shape, not its size; my biggest tuber was 8 in. (20 cm) long by 2 in. (5 cm) in diameter. Some other fingerling varieties, of course, can also grow gigantic.

A strange thing about the appearance of the 'Makah Ozette' is its profusion of deep-set eyes, evenly distributed over each tuber. The big and little fingers look puckered like a hand-tacked quilt. Stranger still is the way the plant grows. Although I planted my tiny tuber in a back corner of the garden, where it competed with nearby shrubs and received little water, the plant grew 5 ft. (1.5 m) tall. And it kept growing into autumn.

It's said that potatoes, like tomatoes, come in both determinate and indeterminate types. The determinate ones die soon after producing their tubers, more or less all at once; the indeterminate ones keep on growing until disease, insect predation, or freezing weather kills their tops. 'Makah Ozette', then, must be indeterminate, and unusually disease-resistant besides. My plant showed no shriveling or discoloration until well into October, after at least a week of steady rain.

Harvest time brought more surprises. First, although the tubers I dug were all close to the surface, they had spread widely from the center of the plant, 18 in. (46 cm) in all directions. What a clever way, I thought, for a tuberous plant to protect its future generations from soil-borne disease. Second, the thin skin of 'Makah Ozette' proved remarkably tough: I could scrub the potatoes immediately after digging without rubbing off any skin. I didn't have to store these potatoes dirty while they hardened off.

The following spring, I didn't need to plant potatoes. Because 'Makah Ozette' potatoes spread so far, it's easy to miss harvesting a few. And because the potatoes resist rot over the winter, new plants come up here and there on their own. And they are healthy. Since my initial planting I've never had to plant 'Makah Ozette' potatoes again, and I've never been without them. They have gone wild in my garden. If they're growing in the shade or if they don't get water, no matter—they will still produce tubers, at least modestly.

Every other potato variety I've raised has grown only about 2 ft. (60 cm) tall, has died back in August, and has kept their baby tubers close to Mom. The tubers have had tender skin and shallow eyes, clustered at one end. The plants have seldom returned on their own in subsequent years, and when they have come back, they have usually been scabby. Why is 'Makah Ozette' so different?

A 2010 DNA study provides the answer: 'Makah Ozette', unlike all the other potato varieties with which I'm familiar, did *not* derive from the Peruvian potatoes brought to Spain in 1570. Those varieties slowly spread through Europe, and eventually Scottish and Irish immigrants brought them to North America. The first permanent North American potato patches were established in New England in about 1719. From there the potatoes spread westward.

But potatoes reached the Pacific Northwest long before the first big wave of American settlers. The Pacific Fur Company planted potatoes near Astoria, Oregon, in 1811, and the Hudson's Bay Company grew potatoes and other vegetables at its forts, beginning with Fort Vancouver in 1825. By that year, however, native tribes in the region were already growing and trading potatoes in large quantities. Among these tribes were the Makah.

The DNA study shows that 'Makah Ozette' is more closely related to Chilean potatoes than to European, North American, or Peruvian cultivars. So are 'Haida' and 'Tlingit' potatoes of Alaska's southern coast, which are nearly identical to 'Makah Ozette'. The researchers conclude that the potatoes reached the Pacific Northwest by ship from Chile, perhaps with a stop in Mexico. The first 'Makah Ozette' may have been brought by the Spanish traders who had a garden with potatoes at Nootka Sound, on the west coast of Vancouver Island, from 1790 to 1792, or by the Spanish explorers who, in 1792, built and briefly occupied a fort at Neah Bay, in Makah territory. Or the potatoes may have come with some earlier, forgotten expedition. Other writers speculate that tribal members themselves brought back the potatoes from a long expedition south by canoe.

In any case, the Makah, like other Northwest tribes, took quickly to the potato. The tribes grew potatoes much as they did camas, and they named this new vegetable after wapato, a water plant whose tubers, harvested by tramping in aquatic mud, taste like potatoes. When fur companies established posts in the region, tribal members traded potatoes as well as pelts for tools, beads, and blankets. In 1854, the ethnologist George Biggs wrote that the Duwamish and other Northwest tribes cultivated about thirty acres of potatoes at the outlet of Lake Washington, and they harvested about three thousand bushels. That's one hundred bushels per acre—the same average yield as for commercial farmers today.

The tribes gave up the potato business when white settlers took over their lands. Some tribes, however, continued planting potatoes in their gardens. The Makah have stewarded their 'Ozette' potato, named for one of their ancient villages, for well over two centuries. Not until the late 1980s did the Makah share the potato with non-natives.

In 2005, 'Makah Ozette' potato was boarded to the Slow Food Ark of Taste, a catalog of endangered foods from all over the world. In 2008 the Makah Nation, Slow Food Seattle, and local farmers together formed a Slow Food "presidium"—a project to safeguard the future of a traditional food by establishing production standards and promoting local consumption. Slow Food Seattle has since worked to secure certified disease-free stock, to share seed and crop potatoes with the Makah tribe and the general public, and to promote the potato in the Seattle area and beyond.

The project has been only somewhat successful. Although the potatoes are freely passed among home gardeners, commercial seed companies can legally sell only certified disease-free seed potatoes, and those have been entirely unavailable in some years. At this writing 'Makah Ozette' seed potatoes are available from the Portland Seedhouse, Irish Eyes Garden Seeds, and Cultivariable, but I've found few other commercial sources. 'Haida' and 'Tlingit' potatoes are even harder to get.

But what, you may ask, does 'Makah Ozette' taste like? Gardeners have variously described the potato as earthy, nutty, firm, creamy, and similar to cooked beans. To me the flesh is starchy, like that of a russet potato, but denser and drier; any nuttiness or beaniness is subtle. Still, I like roasting or ricing 'Makah Ozette' potatoes (ricing works better than mashing, because they are hard to peel completely). The potatoes are delicious boiled whole and dipped in aioli (or seal or whale oil, I suppose, in Makah style), or baked, lightly smashed, and showered with roasted hazelnut oil. French-fried 'Makah Ozette' potatoes turn out crisp on the outside, dry on the inside, and surprisingly rigid; this is the potato for anybody who dislikes limp fries. The potatoes make excellent gnocchi, too.

Along with high productivity and drought- and disease-resistance, good taste is one more reason to try this potato in your garden. I hope you can find it at your local seed swap.

Roasted Potatoes *with* Hazelnut Oil

SERVES 2

This is Robert's favorite way to prepare 'Makah Ozette' potatoes. He varies the recipe by using rosemary, oregano, or sage instead of cumin, olive oil or walnut oil instead of hazelnut oil, and black pepper instead of hot pepper. He sometimes mixes in some thick-sliced onion with the potatoes, and he may add a last-minute sprinkling of Parmesan cheese.

1 pound (454 g) potatoes

2 tablespoons roasted hazelnut oil

½ teaspoon salt

½ teaspoon ground cumin

Pinch of hot pepper flakes

1. Heat the oven to 400°F (200°C). Cut the unpeeled potatoes into 1 in. (2.5 cm) pieces, and put them into a bowl. Pour the oil evenly over the potato pieces, and toss. Add the salt, cumin, and pepper flakes, and toss again to distribute the flavorings uniformly. Spread the mixture in a roasting pan.

2. When the oven is hot, roast the potatoes for 20 minutes. Turn them gently, and cook them for 10 to 20 minutes longer, until they are tender and browned.

The Onion *that* Walks

It was at a rural community festival that I first encountered Egyptian walking onions. I saw the box full of little bulbs on a table where a woman sat still and alone all day, with her one product to sell. It was the name that sold me. I handed her a dollar and took home ten bulbs. That was probably a dozen years ago, and Egyptian walking onions, *Allium ×proliferum*, have been with me ever since. They are a kind of onion that produces no seed—a sterile cross, genetic researchers have determined, between *A. cepa* var. *aggregatum*, the shallot, and *A. fistulosum*, the Welsh or bunching onion. Egyptian walking onions multiply like Welsh onions, into clumps of scallions, hollow-leaved. In summer some of the scallions send up a hollow stalk, as tall as 2 ft. (60 cm), at the top of which appears a white, papery sack. The sack opens, in time, to a cluster of sterile little white onion flowers and tiny green "bulbils," numbering anywhere from two to thirty. The bulbils grow to a maximum size of ¼ to 1 in. (0.5 to 2.5 cm) and develop a papery skin like that of a bulb onion. They may sprout, forming an aerial clump of short scallions. *Those* scallions may then sprout, and a third, even smaller clump of bulbs may form. The cluster—or tiered clusters—of bulbs gets so heavy, if left alone, that the stalk bends to the ground. When the rains come, the bulbils begin to form roots, which bury themselves in the earth. In the spring, a new clump forms about 2 ft. (60 cm) from the old one. A smaller clump may take root some inches farther along. The onion has taken a walk.

The term *walking onion* has been in use only since the start of the twenty-first century. Before that, this onion had many names, most of them apt. It has been called the tree onion and the topset, or top-setting, onion. Because of its unusual hardiness—the plant survives temperatures as low as –30°F (–34°C)—it has also been called the winter onion. Botanists have called it *Allium cepa* var. *viviparum*, because it reproduces through plantlets attached to the parent plant; *A. cepa* var. *proliferum*, because it produces many offspring; and *A. cepa* var. *bulbiferous*, a wonderful name, I think, that needs no explanation.

The walking onion hasn't always been called *Egyptian*. That epithet was in the past applied to the potato onion, a kind of shallot once popular among home gardeners. Neither of these onions came from Egypt. Some writers have speculated that walking onions were called Egyptian because gypsies brought them to Europe, from Egypt or someplace else (the word *gypsy* is derived from *Egyptian*). In fact, the only thing walking onions and Romani have in common is that they travel. But *Egyptian* has an exotic appeal, and exoticism helps sell plants. It worked on me.

If walking onions didn't come from Egypt, I wondered at some point, where did they come from? Louis le Comte, a French Jesuit missionary, saw such onions in China in 1687. The plants he described had as many as four tiers! But apparently he didn't bring home any bulbils.

Walking onions made their next literary appearance, as far as I can determine, in England in 1807. In his *Complete Dictionary of Practical Gardening*, Alexander McDonald claimed that the "Canada tree onion" was native to North America. It is not, but the idea stuck. John Baxter attempted to explain this onion's origin in 1830: In Canada, "where the climate being too cold for onions to flower and seed, they are allowed to throw up flower stalks, the flower becomes viviparous, and bears bulbs instead of flowers." If we discount Baxter's opinion that an onion could spontaneously react to the cold by becoming sterile and viviparous, we must ask if the bulbils, which tend to dry up completely if kept indoors from fall to spring, could have been brought from China to Canada before 1807 and successfully planted in their new home. More likely, I'm guessing, a natural cross between shallot and Welsh onion happened in Canada—or in England!—as it had long before in China, with a similar result.

Such a cross may have happened yet again in Pennsylvania, in the mid-nineteenth century. Or perhaps the first Pennsylvania cross wasn't natural but deliberate. In any case, in a village called Catawissa, F. F. Merceron began improving top-setting onions and promoting them for pickling. He developed strains that grew as tall as 5 ft. (1.5 m) and produced bulbils in three colors: red, yellow, and white. The onions appeared at the 1899 Paris Exhibition as *ciboule Catawissa*—an entirely new species, in the opinion of many. Today the Catawissa strains are among numerous varieties of top-setting onions that are shared among seed savers. "Egyptian Onion," "Tree Onion," "Winter Onion," and "Catawissa Onion" were all popular entries in North American seed catalogs from the 1880s through the 1930s. With the upheaval of the Great Depression and World War II, however, the top-setting onion fell into obscurity. Rebranding it "the Egyptian Walking Onion" seems to have revived gardeners' interest.

The best thing about this onion is that it never dies. The bulbils I share with friends today may be essentially the same plant that was discovered in Canada or Pennsylvania in the nineteenth century. Obviously, the plant resists disease. And there are no seeds to collect and clean and save and replant in spring. "It is the hardest matter in the world to kill them," declared the Cleveland Nursery catalog in 1889. "It has such an inveterate habit of growing that it grows any time when in the ground or out of it," asserted the A. I. Root catalog in 1891.

Opinions on the taste of the onion vary. John Baxter thought it rather strong; "it is more an object of curiosity than use." He was probably referring to the small, shallot-like bulbs that form at the base of a plant at the end of its second season. The heat is no problem if you're not using the onion raw. Besides, the sharpness of the bulbs depends on the time of year, according to Harry Sussman, a Master Gardener. "The bottom part should only be used in early spring and late fall," he wrote in *National Gardening* in 1989. "At these times it has a mild, sweet flavor and is excellent in salads."

For me the scallions matter more than the bulbs. Vaughan's Seed Store, in describing the onion as "very sweet and tender" in 1894, may have been referring to the green shoots. They certainly seem mild to me, though I admit that I seldom eat any scallions raw. However, for someone accustomed to cooking in East Asian styles, it's the abundance and earliness of these scallions, not their flavor, that make them invaluable. They can be dug and used whole or cut like chives or garlic chives, to grow right back up again.

The people perhaps most enthusiastic about the walking onion, the French, seem uninterested in its scallion form. But they love to pickle the larger bulbils in vinegar, like gherkins. The bottom bulbs can also be pickled in this way. Harry

Sussman advised pinching off bulbils as they form to develop larger bottom bulbs in the following year.

For Harry Sussman, the "real crop" was the stem of the plant. In late July he would dig up the clusters, separate the individual plants, and reset them 8 in. (20 cm) apart in rows 12 in. (30 cm) apart. Then, in late October, he would dig up each plant. He would cut off the roots and green top, peel off the outer skin, and leave a clean white piece of stem about 6 in. (15 cm) long. He would use these stems immediately or freeze them for winter meals.

Although I have referred to Harry's article repeatedly over the years, I have never been so systematic as he was in caring for and using Egyptian walking onions. I employ them primarily as scallions, beginning in very early spring. When the clumps get too big or numerous, I dig up some of the onions for their bottom bulbs. If in the fall I have a little space at the front of a border, I plant a few of the bulbils, about 6 in. (15 cm) apart. I may throw some of them, unpeeled, into stock, and I always give some away. If winter comes and forgotten clumps of bulbils begin rooting on the ground, I may replant them. Most of all, I take pleasure in watching the growth of these onions through the summer, as they bend and twist crazily while their aerial bulbils grow and sprout.

Today many nurseries sell Egyptian walking onion bulbils, of various strains. Some bulbils have red skins, some brown. Some are elongated rather than round. Those sold as Catawissa may be bigger than others, or not. For round, red bulbils from someone who truly loves them, see Tracy Paine's website at egyptianwalkingonion.com.

Korean-Style Scallion Pancakes

SERVES 2

For these pancakes I use either whole young walking onions or the leaves (not the stalks) of older walking onions. You can substitute any other kind of green onion; a bunch of store-bought scallions will do fine. Whatever onions you use, cut off any roots, halve the onions lengthwise if they are too long for your pan, and halve them lengthwise if they are too thick to cook quickly.

Koreans add various kinds of vegetables and seafood to their pancakes. Once you get the hang of this recipe, feel free to experiment with other ingredients. I prefer to cook my pancakes in flavorful peanut oil, but you can use any oil suitable for frying. For the sauce, you can use rice or cider vinegar, but I prefer smoky, black Shanxi vinegar, from northern China.

Dipping Sauce

2 tablespoons soy sauce

1 ½ teaspoons vinegar

1 teaspoon sugar

1 garlic clove, minced

½ teaspoon sesame oil

Pinch of hot pepper flakes

Whisk together the soy sauce, vinegar, sugar, garlic, sesame oil, and pepper flakes in a small bowl.

Pancakes

¾ cup (90 g) all-purpose flour

1 tablespoon cornstarch

½ teaspoon fine salt

1 garlic clove, minced

¾ cup (180 mL) ice-cold water

Vegetable oil

2 ounces (57 g) trimmed walking onions, divided

½ cup (125 g) salad shrimp (cooked and peeled tiny shrimp), thawed but very cold (optional), divided

1 large egg, beaten, divided

1. Combine the flour, cornstarch, salt, garlic, and ice water in a bowl, and whisk until the batter is smooth. It should seem just slightly runnier than typical breakfast pancake batter.

2. Heat a 10 in. (25 cm) cast-iron pan over high heat until it is quite hot. Reduce the heat to medium-high, add 1 tablespoon of oil, and swirl the pan to distribute the oil. Pour in half the batter in a spiral so that it spreads evenly around the pan. Lay half the onions—parallel to one another, not overlapping—on top of the batter. Sprinkle half the shrimp, if you are using it, over the batter. Press the shrimp and onions into the batter with a spatula. Drizzle half the beaten egg over the shrimp and onions. Let the pancake cook for about 4 minutes, until the top is partially cooked and you can see a golden color on the bottom when you lift the edge with a spatula.

3. Flip the pancake with a spatula. For more crispness, pour about ½ tablespoon of oil around the edge of the pancake. Press the pancake down with your spatula so that it cooks evenly. Let it cook for 2 to 3 minutes longer, until it has browned on the bottom.

4. Slide the pancake onto a dish or cutting board.

5. Cook a second pancake with the remaining ingredients.

6. Serve the pancakes, whole or cut into wedges, alongside the dipping sauce.

133

Black *and* Blue Tomatoes

Back in the 1990s, a radio interviewer asked me if I had a favorite tomato variety. I couldn't name one. I loved homegrown tomatoes, but to me one variety was as good as another.

Today this memory confounds me. I still can't name a single favorite tomato variety, but I can talk for an hour about my many favorites. In the 1990s, of course, I loved cherry tomatoes. Nearly everyone did, because they generally were, and are, the sweetest and tartest of tomato fruits. And I always grew some bland plum type or other, whose flavor would concentrate with boiling down or drying. But I figured the interviewer wanted to know what large, round red tomato I liked best. I couldn't say, because they were all so similar.

When Spanish conquerors arrived in Mesoamerica, the Maya were growing yellow, red, pink, and white tomatoes of various shapes and sizes. Despite Italians' choice of the name *pomodoro* ("golden apple"), Europeans preferred their tomatoes red, and bred them accordingly. But European breeders also maintained diverse shapes in their tomato lines, including the elongated plum and the *costoluto*, or ribbed tomato. English colonists in America took little interest in the tomato at first. From the mid-nineteenth century on, though,

U.S. breeders worked to perfect just one sort of tomato—large, round, red, meaty, and low in acid. This year's favorites would be crossed to create next year's. Bred away were green shoulders, through a mutation that also reduced the amount of sugar in the fruit. As the tomato gene pool shrank, the fruits grew more and more alike. As a gardener, you would choose a cultivar that promised to produce abundantly in your soil and climate. If one year's crop wasn't up to snuff, the next year you might try another variety. You could bet it wouldn't taste much different.

That was still the situation in the 1990s. But the tomato world was changing fast, even as I gave my interview. In fact, I had already planted my first "black" tomato, the 'Black Krim', from Ukraine. The mixed green and red skin was prone to cracking, but I loved this tomato for its beautiful green and red interior—red in the center, with green gel around the seeds and dark outer flesh. The tomato had good acidity and a complex though mild flavor. I may have looked on it as an oddity at first, but it was truly a multipurpose tomato, as lovely in a salad as in a dark red sauce. I even dried the slices.

Two years later I was growing three black tomato varieties. The purplish skinned 'Black Cherry' had wonderful flavor, with the high sugar and acid typical of cherry tomatoes plus the chocolate note of black tomatoes. It was especially lovely combined with yellow and red cherry tomatoes in a salad. 'Carbon', according to the Tomato Growers catalog, was among the darkest of the blacks, but its skin was actually a blend of pink and green; the magnificent blackness—that is, deep redness—was on the inside of this big, oblate tomato. The flavor was outstandingly rich. 'Black Prince', a Siberian variety introduced by Nichols Garden Nursery, was 2 to 3 in. (5 to 7.5 cm) in diameter, slightly elongated, brick red to green on the outside, deep red on the inside, and very tasty.

This was just my sampling, one summer, of the many black varieties suddenly available in seed catalogs. Where had they come from? In the early days of seed catalogs, U.S. companies never used the word *black* or *brown* in describing their tomatoes—although Thorburn's, in 1893, introduced the 'Terra-Cotta'. Beginning in the late nineteenth century, tomatoes were often described as "purple," especially those developed by A. W. Livingston, but tomato enthusiasts now believe that these fruits were what we call pink today. (Pink tomatoes aren't pink like bubblegum, but nor are they the orangey red of ordinary red tomatoes. This is because ordinary tomatoes have yellow skins, and pink tomatoes have clear skins.) Just one late-nineteenth-century tomato, 'Fejee Improved', was described as "maroon."

And then came the Russians. In 1981, Ron Driskill, a horticulture teacher in Alberta, stimulated interest in Siberian seeds after he found an unusual tomato plant in a local nursery. A visitor from the USSR had smuggled in the seeds, which were of an experimental Siberian variety. Ron called the tomato 'Siberia'. He so liked it that he set up a business to sell its seeds, along with seeds of other cold-resistant vegetable varieties.

In 1989, Bill McDorman, the young founder of Montana's Garden City Seeds, visited Siberia. From the Siberian Institute of Horticulture, he collected more than sixty tomato varieties "of every shape and color imaginable." He smuggled them all back to Montana. As the USSR collapsed, more seed lovers followed in McDorman's footsteps. Kent Whealy, cofounder of the Seed Savers Exchange, an educational nonprofit that sells seeds and coordinates a members' seed exchange, journeyed to Russia three times. He befriended Marina Danilenko, who had recently founded two private seed companies and whose mother was a tomato collector. Kent helped Marina develop her businesses, and she returned the favor. By 1993, Marina had provided Seed Savers Exchange with seeds of 170 Russian tomato varieties.

Black, yellow, pink, and red, the Russian varieties became known for being intensely flavorful. As the many black Russian varieties won special attention, Americans discovered they had black, or blackish, tomatoes of their own. In 1990, a Tennessee man, John D. Green, sent seeds of a dusky tomato to Craig LeHoullier, a tomato adviser to Seed Savers Exchange. Because John claimed his tomato had been grown by Cherokee gardeners for a century, Craig named it 'Cherokee Purple'. "It looks like a leg bruise," said Jeff McCormack, of Southern Exposure Seed Exchange, and so it does, to me, though Craig has described the tomato more appealingly as "dusky rosy purple." People liked its flavor and, I suspect, its name, although its Cherokee provenance was never verified. Today 'Cherokee Purple' is probably the most popular black tomato in the United States.

Meanwhile, William Woys Weaver, a venerable food historian from Pennsylvania, shared his own black tomato seeds, passed down to him by his grandfather, with Baker Creek Heirloom Seeds, in Missouri. One variety was the "maroon" 'Fejee Improved', which many had thought to be lost forever. Another was the 'True Black Brandywine', bred in the 1920s by Dr. Harold E. Martin, by crossing 'Fejee Improved' with 'Brandywine'. He also shared seeds of Thorburn's 'Terra-Cotta'. Although no one would call this orange-brown-skinned tomato black, it clearly has what plant breeders have named the gf ("green-flesh") gene, which prevents the complete breakdown of chlorophyll.

While these black varieties were attracting much interest, freelance breeders in the United States were developing unconventional tomato cultivars of their own. Two California breeders, Brad Gates in Fairfield and Fred Hempel in Sunol, and a Washington breeder, Tom Wagner, were specializing in tomatoes with stunning metallic gold and green stripes. I had already grown Tom's 'Green Zebra' and Brad's 'Pink Berkeley Tie-Dye'. Now these breeders were adding to their palettes all shades of "black"—dark chestnut, rust, violet, mahogany, and bronze. Soon I would plant Brad's 'Large Barred Boar', coppery red with green stripes, and Fred's 'Purple Bumblebee', also striped green. And I would add to my collection of favorites the gorgeous 'Chocolate Stripes', which Al Anderson, of Ohio, had bred from Tom Wagner's 'Schimmeig Creg' and a pink Amish tomato.

And then arose a different sort of black tomato, which, for clarity, I prefer to call blue. This sort of tomato has purple coloring (I'm not making things clear, am I?)—a haze, a blotch, or a nearly complete covering—on the skin, and only on the skin. On yellow- and green-fleshed tomatoes the coloring can appear black. You may have seen such staining on tomatillos, a nightshade relative, but until recently it was nearly unknown in tomatoes. It hadn't arisen as a mutation. Instead, it was attained through crossbreeding with wild tomato species from the tomato's birthplace, the Pacific Rim of South America. 'Purple Smudge', perhaps the first such tomato with a name, was developed through a cross with *Solanum peruvianum*, a native of the Galápagos Islands, Ecuador, Peru, and northern Chile. Texas A&M University donated seeds of 'Purple Smudge' to the USDA seed bank in 1963, and the tomato appeared in the Seed Savers Yearbook in 1984. But it was never widely grown.

Jim Myers started his blue-tomato breeding program at Oregon State University about the year 2000, when one of his students noticed the purple on 'Purple Smudge'. The coloring turned out to be anthocyanins, pigments that had been shown to be anti-inflammatory, antimicrobial, and anti-oxidative. These flavonoids are thought to protect against cardiovascular disease, diabetes, obesity, and vision and nerve problems in humans, though none of the evidence is certain. Tomatoes are full of other health-promoting flavonoids. Most prominent among these, usually, is lycopene, a red pigment, which is thought to benefit the heart and lower the risk of some types of cancer. Yellow tomatoes such as 'Sungold', the super-fruity little cherry, are rich in beta-carotene, which the human body converts into vitamin A. Tomatoes contain other flavonoids, too, such as quercetin, kaempferol, and the flavanone naringenin—all of which are supposed to be very

good for us. But not even black tomatoes have anthocyanins. Jim and his students decided to incorporate them into new varieties.

Other scientists were also attempting to turn tomatoes into "nutraceuticals," foods to be promoted as medicine. In 1998, USDA researchers released three new tomato breeding lines that they claimed contained 10 to 25 times more beta-carotene than typical tomatoes. The scientists had crossed domestic tomato varieties with *Solanum pennellii*, yet another wild tomato from western South America. (I don't know what happened with these new tomatoes; perhaps their flavor wasn't good.) David Francis, a professor of horticulture at Ohio State University, began breeding tomatoes rich in beta-carotene using only the gene pool of the domestic tomato. In New Zealand, meanwhile, the Heritage Food Crops Research Trust discovered that some tomatoes, notably the yellow-orange 'Tangerine' and 'Moonglow', contain an unusual form of lycopene that is more efficiently absorbed by the human body. The group began researching whether such tomatoes can help prevent osteoporosis. Even Tom Wagner, the independent Washington breeder, considered possible effects of his work on public health when he bred for higher protein and lower sugar to help people manage diabetes (this may be why his 'Green Zebra' is not among my favorites; I like sweet tomatoes!).

But no one else was breeding anthocyanins into tomatoes. Jim and his team crossed red tomatoes with hybrids previously created by other researchers, who had used three wild tomato species, *Solanum lycopersicoides*, *S. chilense*, and *S. cheesmaniae*.

Jim's team found that by combining two purple-producing genes they could derive a more intense purple color. They released their first anthocyanin tomato, 'Indigo Rose', in 2012. To distinguish anthocyanin tomatoes from other black and purple varieties, they decided to always include "Indigo" as part of the name. I grew 'Indigo Rose' the same year it was released. It is a large cherry tomato with an eggplant-purple skin and a green patch on the underside, where the sun doesn't shine; the purple develops only through exposure to ultraviolet light. When the tomato ripens, the green patch turns orange-red. My single plant set fruit early, but the fruits hung hard on the vine all summer before finally ripening in early October. Harvest was a bit difficult, since I had to either lie on the ground looking up to see the red patches or else palpate each tomato to determine whether it had softened. Although the fruits looked pretty in mixed-tomato salads, their flavor was uninteresting.

Other gardeners gave similar reports. Jim and his team persisted in their work, however, and in 2014 they released Indigo tomatoes with better flavor, 'Indigo Cherry Drops' and 'Indigo Pear Drops'. 'Indigo Kiwi' followed, in 2017. It has a green interior and, Jim thinks, the best flavor.

In 2017 Jim introduced his first paste tomato, 'Midnight Roma'. He wanted those anthocyanins to be included in sauces, on pizza and pasta and so on. There was a problem, though: Usually people peel tomatoes before canning them. It's certainly possible to make sauce from tomatoes by running them through a blender or food processor, as some home preservers do to retain nutrients from the seeds as well as the skins. But USDA recipes for home canning all require that the skins be removed. None of these recipes has been safety-tested for tomatoes with their skins. And it is really hard to get the USDA to do new research for the benefit of home preservers. I hope Jim will try.

While Jim Myers has carried on his blue-tomato work, other breeders have attempted to create health-promoting tomatoes through genetic engineering. In 2021, Sanatech Seed released 'Sicilian Rouge High GABA', a gene-edited tomato enhanced with GABA, an amino acid and a fad micronutrient in Japan, where GABA is valued for its purported calming and sleep-inducing effects. Beijing scientists have likewise used the CRISPR gene-editing method on tomatoes, to increase their lycopene content five-fold. And British scientists have done Jim one better: They have added two genes from the snapdragon flower to produce an especially anthocyanin-rich tomato. Their tomato is purple inside and out and as full of anthocyanins as blueberries. Having won approval from the USDA, the all-purple tomato was to be introduced in select U.S. markets in 2023.

Jim Myers's varieties are not only *not* genetically engineered; they aren't F1 hybrids, either. Like all the tomatoes developed by Brad Gates, Fred Hempel, and Tom Wagner, Jim's tomatoes are open-pollinated. Because they have been developed through conventional breeding over several generations, their progeny grow true to type. This means that the gardener need buy seeds of these varieties only once. As you harvest your tomatoes, you save their seeds to sow another year, when they will produce tomatoes just like the originals (unless two varieties in your garden have crossed).

But you're not supposed to sell the seeds, not without permission. The university's rights to the Indigo varieties are protected through the USDA's Plant Variety Protection Office, which allows the breeder control of marketing and sales.

For Jim, this protection seemed adequate until Byndweed Beth came along. Jim and his team had shared an experimental variety called OSU Blue, or P20, with a few select breeders. Since OSU Blue hadn't been formally released, it also hadn't been granted Plant Variety Protection. Byndweed Beth, as she aptly identified herself, had somehow gotten her hands on some of the seeds, and she offered them to the public through Dave's Garden online forums. The next year, according to Jim, they appeared in Seed Savers Exchange listings. A blue-skinned tomato was now available for anyone to sell or breed.

Breeders snatched up OSU Blue. Ten years later, Oregon State University had five blue tomato cultivars; other breeders had, in total, forty-five. The Chinese-owned chemical company Syngenta had one; an Italian university had one; a breeder in Belgium another. Tom Wagner had ten, and Brad Gates, most impressively, twenty-three. A week after hearing Jim present this information in a Zoom webinar, I discovered several additional blue cultivars he didn't yet know about.

In 2022 my friend Renata grew Brad Gates's 'Indigo Apple', a productive vine bearing medium-size tomatoes with mostly purple skins and sweet, tart red flesh. Good for Jim Myers! I thought. But then I discovered that 'Indigo Apple' was Brad Gates's creation. Using wild tomato strains, he had bred it to be rich in lycopene and vitamin C as well as anthocyanins.

At this writing, Brad's website (wildboarfarms.com) includes blue-smudged varieties such as 'Afternoon Delight' (yellow with a red center), 'Amethyst Cream Cherry', 'Atomic Sunset' (orange plum), and 'Atomic Fusion' (yellow with green seed cavities). People often call Brad's cultivars—and Tom Wagner's, and Fred Hempel's—heirlooms, perhaps because they seem to have been rediscovered from a psychedelic tomato past. Some of the tomatoes have old-time features, like thin skins and green shoulders. But these tomatoes, especially those with blue skins, are different from any that have come before. "Tomatoes have changed more in the last ten years than they have in their entire existence," writes Brad on his website.

Perhaps, though, these tomatoes are heirlooms of the future. I advise you not to worry whether they are rich in anthocyanins or lycopene or beta-carotene; if they taste good, they are good for you. Because they are so special. I encourage you to clean and dry their seeds and store them in a cool, dry place, so you can plant them again and again and pass them along to your children and grandchildren. If you're not saving seeds already, you might start with tomatoes. And, please, forget about those genetically engineered tomatoes. The world of tomatoes has plenty of variety without them.

Ratatouille

You probably don't need a tomato recipe, but I'll share one that may be useful for its simplicity. I make potfuls of ratatouille every late summer and fall and freeze it to eat all winter. Any color and size of tomato or pepper will work for this recipe, though thin-skinned varieties are preferable, so you don't end up with tough bits of skin floating in your stew. I leave out zucchini, a classic ratatouille ingredient, because I don't like it; include it if you prefer.

For each part onion, by volume, use about two parts eggplants and peppers and four parts tomatoes. (Don't fuss over the proportions; they can vary a lot, with good results.)

Onions

Eggplants

Peppers

Tomatoes

Olive oil

Salt

1. In a large pot, heat a tablespoon or more of oil, depending on the quantity of vegetables. Cook the onions over medium heat until they are just tender. As they cook, cut the eggplants into 1 in. (2.5 cm) chunks. Add them to the pot, and stir. Add more oil if needed; eggplants soak it up. Cook the eggplants for several minutes while you cut the peppers into 1 in. chunks. Add the peppers to the pot, stir, and let the vegetables cook while you cut the tomatoes into 1 in. chunks. Add the tomatoes, and let all the vegetables stew together until the tomatoes have become a sauce for the rest. Salt the ratatouille to taste.

2. Serve the ratatouille hot or cold, or freeze it for later use.

The Longest Beans

I knew I had to start growing long beans after Robert and I bought some in an Asian market and "dry-cooked" them, Sichuan-style—in oil, without water. The dense, chewy texture and deep green color intensified as the beans shriveled, and their mild flavor complemented the strong flavors of pork, soy sauce, garlic, ginger, and sesame oil. Here was a bean with no unpleasant beany flavor or mushiness or sliminess, and with no tendency to fall apart with cooking. I had found my favorite bean.

Like my second favorite, scarlet runner beans, the long bean is not a common bean at all. It is not, in other words, in the genus *Phaseolus*. The long bean, yard-long bean, asparagus bean, or noodle bean is a kind of cowpea (or black-eyed pea), *Vigna unguiculata*.

The long bean's subspecies name, *sesquipedalis*, means it's 1½ ft. (46 cm) long. And it often is. "Yard-long" is an exaggeration, although when the beans are mature the pods may reach 2 ft. (60 cm). A trellis covered with vines bearing long beans is an impressive sight indeed.

The long bean became so wonderfully elongated, apparently, through at least a thousand years of Chinese breeding. This may seem strange if you know that the *Vigna* genus originated in tropical Africa. But various species of *Vigna* came to India during the Neolithic period and spread farther from there. These species include other beans familiar to cooks today, such as mung, adzuki, and urad dal. The long bean is the only *Vigna* bean I know that is grown primarily for eating in pod form.

Long beans are easy to grow if you have a long, warm growing season. You'll need ninety frost-free days. Warm nights help, too. Most years my harvest has been small, perhaps because summer nights in western Oregon are usually chilly. Or, I should say, they *were* chilly. In recent years our nights have been getting warmer and my long-bean harvest much bigger. In 2022 the beans came faster than we could eat them, and I ended up freezing many, even though I'd planted only a single 4 ft. (1.2 m) row.

In hot places like the U.S. Southeast, it's often possible to grow two separate crops of long beans per year or to plant several rows in succession, every three weeks. Neither of those strategies will work where the growing season is as short as mine. The seeds won't sprout when the soil temperature is below 50°F (10°C). But I could extend my growing season, if I wanted, by starting the seeds indoors. Some gardeners let their potted long-bean plants get as tall as a foot before transplanting them.

The plants will benefit from compost worked into the soil and regular irrigation, but they aren't fussy. They will tolerate high heat and humidity and brief periods of drought. Mine have been almost entirely unbothered by pests.

Long beans need a sturdy trellis. Whereas pole varieties of ordinary cowpeas grow to no more than about 4 ft. (1.2 m), long beans easily grow to 12 ft. (3.7 m). But 6 ft. (1.8 m) is tall enough for a trellis if you don't want to have to pick from a ladder. The vines will climb up strings attached to a stout frame, or three to four vines can share a bamboo pole. I use a section of cattle panel supported by steel posts and supplemented with bamboo poles for added height.

Once the soil is warm, long-bean vines grow fast. From one day to the next, you'll notice the growth. When the vines reach the top of your trellis, you might pinch them back. Trimming the side shoots to two or three sets of leaves will also keep the plants from getting too top heavy.

When the vines are several feet tall, pretty, pale purple, pea-like blossoms appear, usually in pairs. The beans usually hang in pairs, too. Pick the beans when they are 12 to 18 in. (30 to 46 cm) long and about a pencil's width wide. Harvest the pods by clipping or twisting them away from the stem. Don't cut the stem, or you'll cut away flower buds that would have produced more beans.

Harvest at least every day to keep the vines producing. Once the pods have turned bumpy with swollen seeds, they are past their prime. Late in the season you'll want to leave those fat pods hanging for next year's seed. Until then, keep picking.

Long-bean seeds and pods come in different colors. The seeds are black, white, or red; the pods are yellow-green, dark green, or purple-red. I mix up my seeds so that red pods grow among the green. The yellow-green ones are a bit more tender than the dark green ones. The red ones, which taste just like the green, keep their color with cooking. This characteristic makes them an especially nice addition to a jar of dilly beans. (When I pickle long beans, I process the jars for ten to fifteen minutes instead of five, to tenderize the beans a bit. They need longer cooking than common beans.)

Long beans have many uses besides dry-cooking and pickling. You can boil the beans and then use them in salads. You can cook them in soups and stews; add them about twenty minutes before the end of the cooking. You can blanch the beans and then stir-fry them. Or stir-fry them first and finish by braising them. Long beans are cut into short pieces for cooking, but you could also try stir-frying them whole, and then curling the beans on the serving dish. Elizabeth Schneider, in the classic *Uncommon Fruits and Vegetables*, suggests tying whole beans into "loose pretzly knots," dipping them in tempura batter, and frying them.

Even if you plan to use your beans whole, you'll want to cut off the hard stem ends when you're ready to cook them. I usually leave the pointed bottom ends alone, though you might trim them for uniformity.

Long beans will keep well in a refrigerator for several days. If you can't use them at least that fast, freeze them. Blanch them in boiling water, plunge them into ice-cold water, and drain them well. Pack them into vacuum bags or zippered freezer bags and store the bags in the freezer. The beans retain their texture exceptionally well after thawing.

Dry-Cooked Long Beans

SERVES ABOUT 4

This is my interpretation of Margaret Gin and Alfred Castle's recipe in *Regional Cooking of China*, my favorite Chinese cookbook. You can use regular green beans in this recipe, although they won't have the same chewy texture. You can also substitute bacon or sausage bits for the chopped or ground pork. If you don't have dried shrimp, leave it out, or substitute chopped small pink shrimp. Fermented black beans are a nice addition. Sometimes I make a meatless version and then top the finished dish with chopped roasted peanuts or cashews.

2 tablespoons dried shrimp

1 ½ pounds (680 g) long beans

1 cup (237 mL) vegetable oil

2 tablespoons unrefined peanut oil

4 ounces (113 g) chopped or ground pork

2 quarter-size slices fresh ginger, minced

1 tablespoon sugar

1 tablespoon soy sauce

½ teaspoon salt

2 teaspoons rice vinegar

1 teaspoon roasted sesame oil

Cooked rice or noodles, for serving

1. Put the shrimp into a small bowl, and cover them with water. Let them soak for 20 minutes. Drain them, reserving the soaking liquid.

2. While the shrimp are soaking, cut the beans into 3 in. (7.5 cm) lengths. In a wok, heat the vegetable oil to 350°F (175°C). Fry the beans in small batches until they begin to wrinkle, about 2 minutes. Remove them to paper towels or newspaper to drain.

3. When all the beans are cooked, pour off the vegetable oil. Add the peanut oil, raise the heat to high, and stir-fry the pork, shrimp, and ginger for 2 minutes. Add the sugar, soy sauce, salt, 2 tablespoons of the shrimp soaking liquid or fresh water, and the beans. Stir-fry over high heat until the liquid has evaporated. Turn off the heat and stir in the vinegar and sesame oil.

4. Serve the beans immediately, with rice or noodles.

Shiso, Red
and Green

I first planted seeds of red shiso to color *umeboshi*, Japanese-style pickled "plums." They are made from *ume*, fruit like small, tart apricots, from the tree *Prunus mume*. Sadly, I've failed to make my *umeboshi* production an annual affair, because I've been unable to find a *P. mume* variety that produces fruit reliably in western Oregon (green-gages, I learned the hard way, are a poor substitute).

But I fell in love with shiso. It is, like basil, an annual herb in the mint family. It grows somewhat bigger than basil, to about 2 ft. (60 cm). The leaves are larger and softer than basil leaves, and heart-shaped. Like basil, shiso comes in two basic colors: green and red-purple. Sometimes the green leaves have reddish undersides. Like basil, too, shiso bears a strong aroma. The scent of the green is sharp and refreshing; it is often described as a cross between mint and basil. The scent of red basil is often described as anise-like. I can't personally identify the anise in the aroma, but the scent is somehow darker than that of green shiso, more reminiscent of sweet spices.

At first I knew this herb only as shiso, the Japanese name. Much later I learned that shiso has a long history in the West—the red type known (unappetizingly to me) as beefsteak plant, and both green and red as perilla. I wondered if I should pronounce *perilla* as if it were Spanish. But, no, it's always "purr-ILL-uh." Shiso has borne this name, I found out, since even before Linnaeus listed it. The plant probably first arrived in Europe in the sixteenth century, when European trade with coastal China began. Native to East Asia and Southeast

Asia, perilla was a common garden herb around the East China Sea. Perhaps it took the name of a Portuguese or Spanish plant explorer named Perilla. By the nineteenth century, though, botanists couldn't account for the name—although the Missouri Botanical Garden Plant Finder says perilla is named for the fruiting calyxes, which look something like tiny drawstring bags (*pera* means "purse" in Latin). Perhaps.

Perilla is the genus name; the species name for shiso used to be *nankinensis*, for the city now called Nanjing; today the species name is *frutescens*, which means "shrubby." I'll focus on the genus now, because multiple species of perilla came to the West, some of them probably by mistake. Wild species, of which there are at least three, can be invasive and can cause respiratory distress in cattle and horses. Unless they have nothing else to eat, livestock avoid perilla. Nonetheless, perilla in general is considered a dangerous weed in the southeastern United States. It's not clear to me whether *Perilla frutescens*—shiso—is itself toxic to livestock, but perilla species are said to hybridize easily. So, the poisonous perilla in a Tennessee pasture may be hard to distinguish from the shiso in your garden.

Perilla was once beloved in the Eastern states. The seeds were sold through catalogs beginning in the 1850s—the decade when nurseries began producing catalogs in quantity—and were probably traded even earlier. J. M. Thorburn, in New York, started selling red perilla in 1856, and green in 1868. In 1873 Thorburn added a "sweet scented" purple variety. The foliage was considered ornamental, especially for "ribbon gardening," for geometrical beds, for growing beside silvery plants such as artemisias and dusty miller, and for bouquets. Perilla remained popular for such uses until flashy coleus cultivars outshone it (today perilla, like coleus, is available in variegated cultivars of three or four colors).

In the early twentieth century, the Oriental Seed Company in San Francisco sold green shiso as "Pepper Green." In this catalog, perilla was described as a food: The leaves were slivered or minced as a seasoning and garnish, as they are in China today. Perilla seed oil also found some use in twentieth-century America; it was imported to the United States for industrial applications before World War II. But otherwise North Americans and Europeans overlooked the many practical uses for shiso.

These uses, in Asia, were both medical and culinary. Shiso has been shown to be antifungal, antibacterial, and anti-inflammatory. Essential oil distilled from the leaves has sedative and anti-depressive effects. Because of these attributes, the plant has been historically used to treat many afflictions, including coughs, lung disease, heart disease, anxiety, infections, and intestinal disorders. Strangely, though, shiso has never entered the Western *materia medica*.

In the kitchen—in Japan, Korea, Southeast Asia, Bhutan, and Nepal—shiso has served as a salad herb and potherb. For its antimicrobial properties as well as its flavor, green shiso is served with sashimi and sushi. The leaves are wrapped around little fishes, meat patties, and pieces of barbecued meat, and they garnish donburi dishes. They are minced and included in meatballs and savory pancakes; slivered, they garnish rice, eggs, and tofu. In Vietnam, green shiso is among the raw herbs that accompany main dishes. In Korea, the leaves are included in banchan (small side dishes), either as a briefly fermented kimchi with chile paste and sesame, or as a soy-sauce pickle with garlic, brown sugar, and minced green onion.

Red shiso has special uses, particularly in Japan. It is used for coloring pickled ginger as well as *umeboshi*. After the *ume* are pickled, the leaves may be dried and then ground into a kind of *furikake*, a nutritious condiment for sprinkling on foods. The red leaves are also preserved for the winter by salting. Both fresh and salted leaves are used in place of nori in *onigiri*, rice balls; they are minced and mixed with the rice and used to wrap it, too. Japanese cooks also make red shiso into a bright-red cold drink for summer: The leaves are boiled in a little water, and then strained out. Sugar and vinegar are added, and this syrup is combined with mineral water or soda water and ice.

Shiso has uses beyond any of these. In Japan and parts of India, the seeds are eaten. The raw oil from the seeds is sometimes used for cooking in Korea; more popular still is the roasted seed oil, which is used for flavoring, much like sesame oil. In industry, the seed oil is used like linseed oil, in paint, varnish, printing ink, and linoleum. The seed oil was once used, in Japan, to waterproof paper umbrellas. The essential oil made from the leaves flavors tobacco and foods, and a sugar derived from this oil is used as an artificial sweetener. It is two thousand times as sweet as sugar.

Korean and Japanese perilla varieties are distinct. True shiso, Japanese perilla, is *Perilla frutescens* var. *crispa*. The leaves are more wrinkled than Korean perilla leaves, with a more serrated edge. Korean and Japanese cultivars taste slightly different, too. Two U.S. seed companies offering both Korean and Japanese shiso cultivars are Kitazawa and Johnny's.

Korean perilla has its own names—*deulkkae* for the plant and *kkaennip* for the leaf. *Kkaennip*, pronounced almost like "catnip," literally means "sesame leaf," so Koreans often translate the word as such. Don't be confused; sesame is a very different, tropical plant. For simplicity, I call every perilla cultivar I've grown shiso.

Growing shiso is easy. Plant the seeds indoors or in a greenhouse about six weeks before your average last frost date. Some people soak the seeds overnight to speed germination. Sow the seeds shallowly, and give them warmth, at least until they sprout. Set the plants in the ground after all danger of frost has passed, 12 in. (30 cm) or more apart. You can direct-sow the seeds instead, if you prefer, but you'll have to wait until the weather warms.

When the plants are about 6 in. (15 cm) tall, start harvesting the leaves as you need them, but don't be greedy until late in the season.

If your growing season is long enough, your shiso plants will produce seed stalks and the seeds will mature and self-sow. But you may still want to start shiso indoors the following year so you'll be able to start harvesting earlier. You can also propagate shiso by rooting cuttings in water or potting soil.

Red Shiso Liqueur

MAKES ABOUT 3 ½ CUPS (828 ML)

I've used shiso in some of the ways mentioned in this chapter, but I've also invented my own uses. I dry red shiso and use it as a warmly aromatic herbal tea throughout the winter. I've also made it into this fragrant, lovely red liqueur. I like this liqueur unsweetened, but if you prefer you might add some sugar.

4 ounces (113 g) red shiso leaves and flowers, rinsed and dried

About 3 ½ cups (828 mL) eau-de-vie or vodka

1. Pack the shiso into a quart or liter jar. Add enough liquor to cover the shiso completely. Tightly close the jar, and leave it to sit in a cool, dark place for 1 month.

2. Strain and bottle the liqueur, and store it in a cool, dark place.

The Mucilaginous Melon

I first learned about watermelon's pale-fleshed cousin while studying traditional ways of preserving regular watermelons. Why, I wondered, did people bother to make the watermelon's thin inner white rind into pickles and sweet preserves when the red flesh and the seeds have much more nutritional value and flavor? What was the attraction of the nearly tasteless white part? And what was the insipid, white-fleshed melon that Southerners called pie melon? Did Southerners really make pies out of a sort of watermelon? Was there a culinary connection between watermelon rind and pie melon?

Soon I was reading about the citron melon, a cousin of the watermelon whose flesh is normally cooked and, in Western cuisine, typically preserved in sugar. The common name is derived from the genus name, *Citrullus*, which was apparently inspired by colocynth, a species whose unpicked ripe fruits look like oranges scattered about on the desert floor. Although colocynth is terribly bitter and violently purgative, it was once the *Citrullus* species best known to Europeans, who tended to be plagued by constipation. Today this fruit is also valued for lowering blood sugar in diabetics.

The citron melon was so named because it looks like a muskmelon, in size and shape, but clearly belongs to the *Citrullus* genus. Nineteenth-century seed catalogs listed it with watermelons but called it "preserving citron" or "citron, for preserves." (Mentioning preserves was necessary because in New Jersey muskmelons, for some reason, were also called citrons.)

The citron melon has little in common with the true citron—an ancient fruit that looks something like a big lemon but is mostly pith, with a bit of sour pulp and a fragrant rind. The citron melon is neither sour nor particularly aromatic, although the flesh bears a light watermelon-like scent. Strangely, though, citron melon shares one characteristic of the citron: copious pectin. The pectin makes the raw flesh of the citron melon viscous and can thicken jams, preserves, and pie fillings.

A citron melon's lack of flavor can be a virtue. Like tofu, citron melon adopts and extends the flavors of other foods with which it is combined. In candied form, citron melon can even imitate true citron. Combine cubes of citron melon with sugar and lemon, cook them long and slow, drain off the syrup, let the fruit pieces dry, and you will have chewy little golden pieces of candied fruit that can stand in for candied citron in your fruitcakes.

Although today the citron melon is little known in the United States (except where it grows as a weed), Americans have been cultivating and cooking it for a long time. In 1865, Mrs. S. G. Knight, of Massachusetts, published a detailed recipe for citron melon preserves in her cookbook *Tit-Bits; or, How to Prepare a Nice Dish at a Moderate Expense*. The recipe was much like more modern ones except that the melon was left in long slices. Mrs. Knight didn't explain what a citron melon was. She expected her readers to know.

Like colocynth and the rest of the watermelon genus, citron melon hails from Africa, but how exactly this melon originated is unclear. Taxonomists struggle to divide *Citrullus* into distinct species. Colocynth comes from northwestern Africa. Egusi melon (*C. mucosospermus*), with big, soft seeds that can be hulled between the fingers, comes from West Africa. Watermelon, called *C. lanatus* (Latin for "woolly") because of the texture of its young stems and leaves, is now thought to have developed in northeastern Africa; a possible progenitor is the Kordofan melon of Sudan, with its striped skin and sweet white flesh. *Citrullus* species are most numerous in southern Africa, where taxonomists identify four. Citron melon was until recently thought to be a subspecies of watermelon, *C. lanatus* var. *citroides*, but now it is considered a cultivar of *C. amarus*—a southern African species named for its bitterness. Depending on whom you ask, *C. amarus* may or may not be tsamma melon, a cherished source of water, oil, protein, and even greens in the deserts of southern Africa.

If citron melon is a cultivar of *Citrullus amarus*, how did it lose its bitterness? Or has it really lost its bitterness? Transported around the world by the Spanish, the melon grows wild today in many hot places, including the southern United States, from California to Florida, and much of Australia. Green Deane, an expert forager, describes citron melons growing in abandoned Florida citrus groves. Some taste bland, others bitter. Australians describe the melons growing in cow paddocks and along roadsides. Often these melons are too bitter for any critters to eat, and sometimes they are just a little bitter, around the seeds. Australians call the bitter melons paddy melons and the bland ones jam melons.

Citron melons vary in ways other than bitterness. Although they are usually small, in Australia they may grow to thirty pounds and more. As early as 1885, a Philadelphia seed company offered a "Colorado preserving melon" that could grow as big as forty pounds. Citrus melons vary in shape, too, from round to oblong. And the seed color varies, from white to red to brown to black.

It's unclear to me whether this variability is characteristic of *C. amarus* or caused by crossings between *Citrullus* species. Such crossings occur rather easily. In the U.S. South, pie melons that are oblong and slightly sweet are obvious crosses between citron melons and watermelons. An amateur breeder in Colorado is crossing citron melons and watermelons just by planting the two together and letting the insects do their thing, in hopes of developing a sweet watermelon especially tolerant of drought and poor soil. Colocynth grows wild both in the U.S. South and in Australia, and so colocynth-citron melon crossings may be responsible for the fact that pie melons and paddy melons are often too bitter to eat.

Reading about citron melon made me curious enough to try growing it. I found 'Red-Seeded Citron Melon' listed in the Seed Savers Exchange catalog and sent for some seeds.

That summer my single citron melon vine produced several round fruits, each no more than 8 in. (20 cm) in diameter and striped dark green on a pale green background. I picked the melons at the first frost of the year, in early October, and hoped that they would keep well on the cool tile floor of our entry hall while I spent the next several weeks canning and drying tomatoes, peppers, apples, and pears.

One of my blog readers suggested that I read an article by a writer in southern France concerning "jamming melons," or *melons d'Espagne*. In Médoc, wrote Mimi Thorisson, everybody made confiture with these melons just after harvest, in early November. She suggested two variations on the basic confiture, one with vanilla and one with mandarin orange and ginger. Her recipe, I noticed, closely resembled American recipes for citron-melon preserves. In her photos, the *melons d'Espagne* looked just like my citron melons.

I consulted other French sources. In different parts of France, the citron melon goes by different names: *gigérine*, *citre*, *méréville*, and *pastèque à confiture*, among others. Some writers said the melons are harvested in late fall and kept in a cool place until right after Christmas, when they are made into the last preserves of the year. All the French recipes I found were much like both Mimi's and the American recipes. If melons d'Espagne and red-seeded citron melon weren't exactly the same cultivar, I concluded, they must be very close.

In December, I cut into one of my melons. Inside, it fit the French descriptions. The flesh was pale green and bland tasting. It felt slimy. The red seeds were many, large, and hard in comparison with seeds of the sweet watermelon cultivars I knew. To cut the slippery fruit as safely as possible, I turned the halves face down and sliced them straight downward. Then, using a smaller, thinner blade, I cut the rind from the slices without much trouble.

Now I needed to remove the numerous seeds. I poked out as many as I could with the tip of a knife. Then I cut the slices into smaller pieces and poked or pried out more seeds. This is a job to do while listening to an excellent radio program or podcast, so you don't start dwelling on the question of what your time is worth.

I made the melon into preserves, devising my own recipe from the many examples available and including lemon, clementine, vanilla, and a splash of dark rum (ginger would be a good alternative to the vanilla). The preserves turned out much like watermelon-rind preserves—translucent bite-size morsels, solid but tender, in a thick, clear syrup. Citron melon preserves will surprise and delight someone who has never tried such a treat and induce nostalgia in anyone who has.

In February I cut into a second citron melon. Although these melons are notorious for their hard rinds, I'd had no trouble cutting the first one. This time the rind seemed to have toughened. I sympathized with the writer of a poem, published in the Burra, Australia, *Record* in 1935, that begins this way:

> *There ain't no dish I'd rather try*
> *Than my dear wife's good melon pie.*
> *I get a melon from the pit*
> *And take the axe and open it.*

Instead of using an axe I employed my 12 in. (30 cm) chef's knife, which Robert had bought me for cutting big winter squashes. I've been a little bit scared of this knife ever since the day it flew into the air and I caught it by the blade instead of the handle. Since that incident, I had used the knife by holding it in place and pounding it with a rubber hammer. This worked to split the melon cleanly. Besides growing a tougher skin, the melon had also become more mucilaginous, as if someone had injected it with a quart of aloe juice.

This time I made a compote, a dish of fruit cooked in syrup. Citron-melon compote recipes, I'd found, were much more common than citron-melon pie recipes, because the pie is just compote heaped in a baked pie shell (you might need to thicken the liquid, by simmering it a bit, before spooning the compote into the pie shell). The fruit's mucilaginous texture remains after baking, but I don't find it objectionable. In fact, I think the citron melon's greatest charm is its texture when cooked. Sweetened and cooked, citron melon tastes much like a good cooking apple, baked in a pie with some starch added.

I studied two recipes for compotes, one in Mildred Maddocks's *Pure Food Cook Book*, published in New York in 1914, and one by an unnamed cook in Queensland, who described the fruit as "So country! So winter! So not dinner party material."

I based my recipe less on Mildred's than on the Queenslander's, which included, enticingly, cinnamon and marsala. Lacking marsala, I used brandy. I've since tried adding ginger, either along with cinnamon or in place of it, and I like the result just as well. Because the melon is virtually tasteless, all the flavor of the dish comes from the added flavorings—the raisins, brandy, spices, and citrus. How could a dessert with those flavors be anything but good?

Baked Citron-Melon Compote

SERVES ABOUT 8

Making citron-melon compote is an easy way to start playing with this strange, old-timey fruit. If you find the compote too prosaic on its own, you might make it into a pie, perhaps with a topping of cream or meringue. But I like this old-fashioned dish just as it is, for breakfast or an afternoon or late-evening snack—and maybe even as a homey dinner-party dessert.

For this recipe, you'll need a melon that is about 8 in. (20 cm) in diameter, or you can substitute two smaller melons. Note that the raisins require several hours of soaking in the brandy.

½ cup raisins

¼ cup brandy

One 5 pound (2.27 kg) citron melon

1 cup (200 g) sugar

1 orange

1 lemon

1 teaspoon ground ginger (optional)

2 cinnamon sticks

2 tablespoons (28 g) butter

1. Put the raisins into a small bowl, and pour the brandy over them. Let them soak for several hours.

2. Cut the melon in half, and cut each half into narrow wedges. Poke or pry out the seeds. Peel each wedge with a knife, and then cut the wedge into 1 in. (2.5 cm) pieces. Heat the oven to 300°F (150°C).

3. Remove the zest from the orange and lemon in fine strips, and then squeeze out the juice, picking or straining out any seeds.

4. In a 3-quart casserole dish, combine the raisins, their soaking liquid, the melon cubes, the sugar, the orange and lemon juices and zests, and the ginger, if you're using it. Tuck the cinnamon sticks into the mixture, and dot with the butter. Bake the compote uncovered for about 2 hours, turning the fruit gently a few times, until the melon is tender, golden, and slightly translucent.

5. You can serve the compote warm or cool, perhaps with cream, though I like it plain.

Maize *for* Meal

When my husband and I left our farm to settle in the town of Lebanon, I figured I would give up growing corn. Corn takes substantial space, and I knew I could buy fresh sweet corn locally—although I always struggle to find varieties that taste more like corn than sugar.

But a few years after the move I missed having my own corn. I don't mean sweet corn; I missed meal corn. Corn for drying and grinding and making into polenta, spoonbread, and the like.

On the farm I had grown Carol Deppe's 'Cascade Ruby-Gold', with good results. Bred here in the mid–Willamette Valley, this variety produces single-color ears in red, red-brown, gold, and maple-gold. Unaware that Carol recommends separating the colors for best enjoyment of their distinct flavors and colors, I had mixed the dry kernels I harvested. My polenta turned out yellow with red flecks, but it was still beautiful to me, and delicious.

'Cascade Ruby-Gold' is a flint corn, as opposed to a flour corn or dent corn. All three of these basic types are loosely called field corn, but they differ in the makeup of the endosperm, the part of the kernel that serves as a food store for the developing embryo. Part of the corn endosperm is soft and floury, and part is hard and flinty. Flour corn kernels are mostly the former, and flint corn kernels are mostly the latter. Dent corns originated in crosses between the two.

Flour corns are the types grown in Mexico and the Southwest for making tortillas. Before they are ground into masa, these corns are first nixtamalized— that is, heated in water with calcium hydroxide (pickling lime, or *cal*), a process that turns the corn kernels into hominy. Nixtamalization also transforms the flavor of the corn, makes niacin available to the human body, and releases pectin, which helps hold tortillas together. Nixtamalizing corn is easy to do at home, though grinding the resulting hominy can be a bit more difficult.

But flour corns are useful without nixtamalization. They can be simply ground into soft flour for making fine-textured breads and cakes.

Because autumn rains can cause flour corns to rot, they aren't typically grown in northern, wetter regions. But Carol has developed one variety, 'Magic Manna', that dries early enough in the season to escape the fall rains. I will probably try it, one of these years.

Flint corn is easily identified by the very hard, round exterior of each kernel. The flinty part of the endosperm helps protect the ears from autumn rain and enables them to survive freezes. When you grind this corn, the meal turns out gritty. The grit provides an appealing texture in products made with the meal, as long as it is cooked with plenty of liquid and for an adequate length of time. I like flint corn mainly because I love polenta.

Dent corns are traditionally grown in the Southeast and Midwest. Each kernel has a floury column in the center that is ringed by flinty endosperm. Because the floury part contracts more when it dries, a dent appears at the top of the kernel. Dent corn is more suitable for cornbread than for flour or polenta. Dent varieties known as "garden corn" were once popular for roasting, but today most dent corn is dried and used industrially, for livestock feed, oil, ethanol, syrup, starch, and so on. There are non-hybrid, traditional dent varieties, but, even so, dent corn hasn't particularly interested me.

I wanted to grow flint corn again. So I signed up for a community garden plot.

The corn that attracted my eye in the seed catalogs was 'Glass Gem'. It is an "Indian corn," that is, a decorative variety with multicolored ears (through the nineteenth century, by the way, *all* maize was called Indian corn). Looking like little glass beads, the kernels appear in various shades of blue, green, pink, red, yellow, and white. A half-Cherokee man from Oklahoma, Carl Barnes, bred the original version, in the 1980s, from a mix of old Native American varieties. His friend Greg Schoen crossed the "rainbow corn" further with Southwestern flour corns, to "strengthen the genetics," Greg explained, because inbreeding makes corn plants grow smaller and weaker over time. In 2008 Greg began sharing 'Glass Gem' freely. Since then, seed companies have been selling out early in the season. Gardeners all over the country have gone wild for 'Glass Gem'.

The packet I ordered held enough seed to plant a small block, about 9 by 9 ft. (2.7 by 2.7 m). The seeds sprouted quickly, and the stalks grew tall, to about

12 ft. (3.7 m). But then they were slow to form ears, and by the time they did the stalks were sprawling toward, or on, the ground. It hadn't occurred to me to consider the number of days this variety was supposed to take to reach maturity—100 to 110—since our summers had always been long enough for sweet corn. In any case, the advertised growing period wasn't accurate for my garden; I planted in May and couldn't harvest until October and November. Probably the cool, wet month of June slowed growth. Perhaps the stalks fell over because I planted the seeds too close together, or perhaps our normal fall winds were too strong for this corn. Maybe I used too much compost or watered too often. I realized that I had planted Southwestern corn without knowing how to grow it or whether I even *could* grow it well in western Oregon.

The 'Glass Gem' ears turned out small, bigger than the average size of popcorn ears but considerably smaller than typical sweet corn, dent corn, or flint corn ears. Was 'Glass Gem' a kind of popcorn? Popcorn is flint corn with very hard, small kernels. The moisture inside each kernel causes expansion, until the kernel explodes. But "the popping is only marginal," says Greg Schoen about 'Glass Gem', "and the colors do not survive the process."

I shucked the ears and dried them on our basement pool table (well covered to protect the felt), turning them occasionally. A few ears were moldy and some others hadn't fully developed, so I threw them away. Still, in early March I shelled out nearly a gallon of kernels. Most were blue, but I could see the whole rainbow of colors for which 'Glass Gem' is famous.

I tried popping the kernels, with less than marginal results. Thinking they might be too moist, I dried some kernels further in the convection oven, with only the fan running. Still only a few popped, weakly. Eating the semi-popped kernels could break your teeth. 'Glass Gem', I confirmed, made abysmal popcorn.

But I was satisfied: I had my own flint corn for polenta. The meal was a bit grayish, but it cooked up tasty and yellow.

Robert and I are not big eaters of corn in any form; for us it is an occasional treat. So a gallon of corn kernels—which when ground becomes almost a gallon and a half of meal—lasts us at least a year. We can keep the whole kernels even longer, if we like, because the oil, protected within, will not go rancid. I grind the corn as we need it, easily and quickly, in the Vitamix.

During the COVID-19 pandemic, wheat flour disappeared from the supermarkets in our area. If we hadn't been buying whole wheat in 25 lb. (11.3 kg) bags, we might have had to give up wheat altogether for a while. But we could have made do for weeks, at least, on our homegrown corn and potatoes.

"Field" corn, then—flint, dent, or flour—can be a survival food for gardeners. Wheat is an impractical crop to plant in a small yard, but corn can produce the same amount of grain in a third of the space. From a 12 by 12 ft. (3.7 by 3.7 m) plot of 'Cascade Ruby-Gold' or another variety appropriate to your climate, you should be able to reap one to two gallons of dry corn. Corn for drying is easy to grow and harvest and store. And it is especially nutritious, because, unlike supermarket cornmeal, it retains its germ, which is rich in vitamin E, minerals, and polyunsaturated fats, and its seed coat, which is full of fiber.

Here are some tips for producing your own corn for drying:

- Choose a variety that is bred for your purpose and adapted to your region, and whose ears will dry on the stalks before the rains come.
- If you're planting a later variety, soak the seeds before planting to help them sprout faster, or start them indoors in small pots and then transplant the seedlings to the garden.
- Plant in a block rather than a long row, because corn doesn't pollinate itself but depends on the wind to carry pollen from one plant to another.
- If birds are eating your seedlings, cover the whole block with floating row covers.
- To shell your corn, try twisting the ears to loosen the center kernels, and then push off several kernels at a time with your thumb (you will probably want to wear gloves). Carol Deppe says she breaks ears in half and rubs them together. I've found a bamboo scraper helpful, but with it the corn tends to go flying. I use a deep container, try to keep my hands positioned to catch kernels that would otherwise fly, and pick up the flyers afterward.
- If shelling corn hurts your hands, consider buying a tool. The simplest corn sheller is a ring with ridges on the inside that you twist over the cob. A polyethylene sheller costs about five dollars, a metal type eight to twenty dollars. The regular size is too wide for 'Glass Gem', but a popcorn-size sheller might work with this variety. For fifty to ninety dollars, you can buy a fast, cast-iron, hand-cranked sheller into which you insert the whole ear.
- Consider freezing shelled corn for a few weeks, as Carol Deppe does, to kill any insects in it. But insects are more of a problem with flour corn than dent corn. I don't freeze my dent corn, and I haven't had any problems with insects.

Robert's Carrot Cornbread

SERVES ABOUT 8

My husband developed this recipe out of his love for Indian spices. He used his homemade *panch phoron*, a Bengali mix of fennel, brown mustard, nigella, fenugreek, and cumin seeds. I don't know whether he intended the carrots to be another Indian touch, but their inclusion makes the cornbread moist as well as fragrant. Though it isn't sweetened, it reminds me of carrot *halwa*, a northern Indian dessert.

I've made this cornbread with 'Cascade Ruby-Gold' as well as 'Glass Gem' flint corns, both with good results. I grind the dry corn in a Vitamix blender.

Using purple rather than orange carrots makes the cornbread appear to be flecked with blueberries.

Butter or oil, for greasing the pan

1 cup (120 g) all-purpose flour

1 cup (160 g) fine-ground whole cornmeal

1 teaspoon salt

2 teaspoons aluminum-free baking powder
(such as Rumford)

2 teaspoons panch phoron
(or your own similar spice mix), ground

2 eggs, beaten

1 cup (237 mL) milk

¼ cup (57 g) sour cream

½ cup (113 g) butter, melted and briefly cooled

1 cup (110 g) finely grated carrots, packed

1. Heat the oven to 350°F (175°C). Grease an 8 to 9 in. (20 to 23 cm) square pan or a 10 in. (25 cm) round pan.

2. Sift the flour, cornmeal, salt, baking powder, and panch phoron into a bowl. Stir in the eggs, milk, and sour cream. Fold in the butter, followed by the shredded carrots. Spread the mixture in the greased pan. Bake the cornbread for 35 to 40 minutes, until a toothpick inserted in the center comes out clean.

169

Chicory Reborn

*T*he most exciting Valentine's gift I've ever received was a box of bitter winter vegetables. Don't get me wrong; I am always grateful for a gift of good dark chocolate. But giving me a box of chocolates is like giving a smoker a pack of cigarettes. Finding a big box of Belgian endives on the porch was a joy in part because it was totally unexpected.

Besides, I'd never tasted this sort of vegetable before. I hadn't grown it myself—raising Belgian endive is a special project, as I'll explain—and I tend to pass by supermarket vegetables that sell for nearly ten dollars a pound, as Belgian endive often does, when you can find it at all. In fact, endive was so foreign to me that talk of it or any of its forms or relations used to send me running flustered to the dictionary.

In case you're confused, too, let me try to sort out the nomenclature associated with this plant. What we call Belgian endive is actually chicory—or succory, as English speakers used to call it—a plant of the genus *Cichorium*, recognizable along roadsides in the United States and Europe by its startlingly blue, daisy-like flowers, which shrivel unhappily when you pick them. Dig up the plant, and you'll find a long white root that you can roast and grind to make a bitter, caffeine-free coffee adulterant or substitute.

The genus *Cichorium* comprises two or more species, depending on how botanists sort the various forms, and a lot of subspecies. *C. endivia* includes curly endive—or, to *les snobs, frisée* (French for "frizzed")—with curled, deeply toothed leaves, and a form with broader, flatter leaves often called escarole. Belgian endive isn't true endive but a very similar relative, *C. intybus,* which when grown from seed in the garden produces bitter, green, dandelion-like leaves. After these leaves are

171

removed in the fall, the root, stored in darkness under particular conditions, will produce a pale, mild-flavored head of Belgian endive. The heads are also known in English by their Flemish name, *witloof* ("white-leaf") chicory. In French, Belgian endive is sometimes called *endive*—"on-DEEV," a pronunciation now fashionable in the United States—but more often *chicon*.

Radicchio, you might think, is simply a colorful Italian form of Belgian endive. But the original radicchio, 'Rosso di Treviso', began as a cross between *Cichorium intybus* and *C. endivia*, and the other popular cultivars were bred from this original. 'Rosso di Treviso'—in its early, *precoce* form—looks like a deep-red-and-white version of its gold-and-white Belgian cousin (*tardivo* is late Treviso radicchio, sold after the heads have opened and turned more bitter). 'Rosso di Chioggia' is a rounder version of Treviso radicchio, and 'Variegato di Castelfranco' looks like a pale, red-flecked head of butter lettuce.

In the United States, nearly all Belgian endive was once imported. That changed in 1983, when Rich Collins started a company now called California Endive, in Rio Vista, California. Rich is the man who sent me my box of Belgian endives—two years in a row, in fact. To promote his products, he was shipping Valentine's packages of chicons, with and without their roots, to food writers and chefs around the country. "Ten million Belgians can't be wrong!" was Rich's slogan.

Thanks to Rich Collins, Belgian endive is no longer a seasonal food; the company produces it year-round. At the growout facility in Rio Vista, the collected roots are kept in cold storage until needed and then packed upright into big trays, which are stacked in a big, dark, temperature-controlled room and watered and fed hydroponically. Some Italian farmers use a similar method for growing radicchio.

California Endive now sells more than four million pounds of Belgian endive per year, including not only the original, pale type but also what the company calls red endive, a cross of Belgian endive with Treviso radicchio. Today California Endive is the world's largest producer of red endive.

The day I received Rich's first box of chicons, my daughter, Becca, and I used three of them in a salad like one she remembered from Belgium, where she had lived for a year during high school. We cut off the base—about ⅛ in. (3.2 mm)—of each chicon, cut out the core to a depth of about ½ in. (1.25 cm), and sliced each chicon crosswise. We tossed the slices with apple chunks and toasted chopped walnuts, and then dressed the salad with cider vinegar, walnut oil, and a little salt and honey. The pleasantly crisp chicory was only slightly bitter, less bitter than the walnuts, and the sweetness of the apples and honey

balanced the bitterness of both the nuts and greens. I could imagine other sweet foods taking the place of the apples: orange sections, slivered fennel, pomegranate berries. Lemon juice could substitute for the vinegar. For a less bitter salad, hazelnuts could replace the walnuts. Fatty foods—bacon, cheese, or avocado—could damper the bitterness even more. In Belgium, Becca said, the dressing would be mayonnaise.

She tried such variations. In fact, she and my husband used the entire first boxful of Rich's Belgian endive in tossed salads before I had a chance to experiment with the lovely red and gold heads.

I wanted more Belgian endive. I found it in two markets, but the prices put me off. Could I grow my own instead?

Although California Endive was—and still is—the only major U.S. producer of Belgian endive, here and there people were growing chicons seasonally, for local sales or household use, using more primitive methods. In search of instruction, I consulted the catalog for Nichols Garden Nursery, which offered the hybrid witloof 'Zoom': "Sow in the open May-June, lift and trim roots in late fall. Place upright in a bucket filled with sand or sawdust. Provide warmth and moisture for 1 to 3 weeks, and you can begin to harvest." Other writers elaborated. Frann Leach, a blogger in Edinburgh, Scotland, wrote that at harvest time in late fall she kept only the roots that were thick and not "fanged" (forked). Trim the leaves to 1 in. (2.5 cm), Frann recommended, and store the roots horizontally, covered with sand, in boxes in a shed or outdoors covered with straw. To force the roots, Frann said, trim them to a uniform length of 7 to 8 in. (18 to 20 cm) and stand them in a pot filled with aged compost, soil, or sand at a temperature of 50 to 64°F (10 to 18°C). Euell Gibbons weighed in, too, I found, in *Stalking the Wild Asparagus*. Be sure the crowns just show in the soil packed around the roots, wrote Euell, and then cover them in at least 18 in. (46 cm) of sawdust, and water as needed. Euell grew his witloof in a box; Frann used a flowerpot, and upturned a second pot as a cover, blocking the drain holes to exclude all light. You can instead plant the roots in a greenhouse or cold frame, Frann said; in this case, cover them with 8 in. (20 cm) of soil, sand, or leaf mold.

Nichols Garden Nursery was, conveniently, just a twenty-minute drive from home. I stopped by for some 'Zoom' seeds. I would plant my first chicory crop in just a few weeks.

In the spring I planted some of the seeds in the garden. They sprouted readily and formed big, ferociously bitter loose heads. Neither the deer nor I were tempted to eat them. By leaving them alone, we ensured that the plants would have the energy to form big roots.

In December I dug up the roots, trimmed off their tops, and took the roots to the barn. I found a plastic box, 13 in. (33 cm) deep and cracked on the bottom, which seemed a perfect planting container; nobody would mind my filling a broken box with dirt, and the roots would have drainage, if needed, without my damaging the box further. Lacking both sand and light soil as possible planting mediums, I used some commercial potting mix that I had on hand. I trimmed off the bottoms of the roots so that the tops would be covered with at least 1 in. (2.5 cm) of the moistened potting mix. Now I needed to bury the roots farther in a light material like sawdust or leaf mold, or more planting mix, but I had already filled the box to the top. I piled some wheat straw over the roots, inverted another plastic box on top, and weighted it with a couple of half-bricks.

Except for occasional peeks, I left the roots alone. Our cat Daphne, however, did not. While we were on vacation in late February, she managed to knock off the bricks and the top box, leaving the chicons barely covered with straw for as long as six days. When we came home, I covered them again—until perhaps a week later, when I found my chicons ready to eat. The biggest, I saw, had grown on the biggest roots. Some of the heads were a bit greener and more open than they should have been, because of Daphne's transgression, or the transparency of the bottom box, or my failure to bury the roots deep enough, or a combination of these possibilities. But no matter—most of the heads were firmly closed, and even the green leaves had hardly any bitterness.

By that time, my California sweetheart farmer, Rich Collins, had come through once again with a Valentine's bouquet of Belgian endive, so harvesting my own chicons simply allowed me to continue the kitchen experiments I'd already begun.

First, I tried the chicons as finger food. Caterers must love Belgian endive leaves; shaped like little canoes, they elegantly transport soft foods—just enough for a couple of tidy bites—from platter to mouth. I cooked small white beans with garlic and sage, flavored the rinsed beans with white wine vinegar, olive oil, a little salt, and chopped chives, and heaped the drained beans into Belgian endive leaves. What a lovely way to serve a bean salad! Next time, I thought, I might add bits of pimiento for color.

I filled more endive boats with Oregon shrimp—the tiny, wild shrimp that come cooked, shelled, and frozen. I mixed a half-pound of thawed shrimp with a tablespoon of minced chives and about three tablespoons of mayonnaise, which I made from roasted hazelnut oil, garlic, lemon juice, and a little pre-pared mustard. Next time I'd sweeten the mixture a bit, maybe with tomato paste in place of the mustard.

Finally, I got around to cooking some of the chicons. Europeans, who are still the main consumers of blanched chicory, mainly eat it cooked. I first followed a method described by Ruth Van Waerebeek in her *Everybody Eats Well in Belgium Cookbook*. You braise the chicons in water and lemon juice with sugar and butter for at least thirty minutes, until they're "tender as but-ter," as Ruth's mom says. Then you reduce the sauce to a syrup while turning the chicons. However odd Ruth's recipe may sound to Americans, given our penchant for barely cooked vegetables, I urge you to try it. The warm, soft, caramelized chicons are truly luscious.

A lot of Italian radicchio recipes—those most favored by American cooks, at least—involve grilling or pan-frying. I chose an Italian recipe that called for wrapping radicchio, quartered lengthwise, with pancetta, but I substituted thin-sliced bacon, which I wrapped as tightly as I could in a spiral pattern. I heated a little olive oil in a pan and cooked the chicon quarters on all sides until the bacon was brown and crisp. Then I put the chicon quarters on a platter, poured off most of the grease from the pan, and added a few tablespoons of balsamic vinegar. I then reduced the sauce by half and poured it over the chicons.

The recipe I started with was more complicated; I was supposed to pickle some red onions, put them on the platter with the chicons—that is, the pancetta-wrapped radicchio—and sprinkle chopped rosemary over everything. But my version had plenty of flavor. And although my bacon-and-balsamic chicons would be out of place on a Belgian table, the Belgian and Italian recipes aren't so different. Both use caramelized sugar and fat to balance the bitterness of the chicory.

Here are a few more ways to use blanched chicory: Purée it to make a creamy soup. Sauté it and add it to risotto. Batter and fry the leaves. Slice and sauté the chicons, and layer the pieces in lasagna or add them to a ham-and-cheese quiche. Braise chicons with chicken in beer (a very traditional Belgian dish). Stuff individual leaves with goat cheese and herbs. For more ideas, see the *Everybody Eats Well in Belgium Cookbook*, or look up *radicchio* in an Italian cookbook.

But remember that chicory remains bitter, however well it is blanched and larded and sweetened. It is a grown-up taste. "You have to learn to appreciate this vegetable," says Ruth Van Waerebeek, "and it is perhaps better not to introduce it to children."

Flemish-Style Belgian Endives

SERVES 4

This is my interpretation of Ruth Van Waerebeek's recipe.

5 tablespoons soft butter, divided

6 to 8 chicons, cored

1 ½ tablespoons lemon juice

1 tablespoon superfine sugar

½ cup water

Salt and freshly ground black pepper

3 tablespoons minced parsley, for serving

1. Smear 4 tablespoons of the butter in the bottom of a large pot. Place the chicons in a single layer, and add the lemon juice, sugar, water, and salt and pepper to taste. Cut a round of parchment paper to just fit inside the pot. Spread the remaining 1 tablespoon butter over one side of the paper, and lay the paper over the chicons, buttered-side down. Place a ceramic plate on top of the paper, cover the pot with a lid, and place the pot over medium heat. Cook the chicons until they are very tender, 30 to 45 minutes, turning them halfway through the cooking. (Take care not to boil off all the water; add more if needed.) The paper and plate together will keep the chicons well bathed in steam.

2. Remove the plate and the parchment paper from the pot, and increase the heat to medium-high. Cook the sauce to a dark syrup, turning the chicons to caramelize them on all sides. Serve them sprinkled with the parsley.

Homemade Chicory Coffee

*A*fter I'd used up all the *chicons* that Rich Collins had sent me, I couldn't bring myself to throw their half-pound roots in the compost. The chicory cultivars preferred for blanching today are distinct from those preferred for coffee ('Magdeburg' is the usual coffee cultivar), but the chicon and coffee varieties are closely related, with thick, fleshy roots. I had to try grinding and roasting my gift roots for chicory coffee.

Coffee blended with chicory became popular in Europe when the naval wars following the French Revolution drove up the price of pure-bean brew. The taste—or, perhaps more accurately, tolerance—for coffee-chicory blends spread from France to the Creoles of New Orleans. New Orleans groceries have sold coffee blended with chicory as well as ground chicory root on its own for as long as anyone remembers. But many natives say that chicory is tolerable at no more than 20 percent in a blend, and then only when the coffee is drunk with milk.

Chicory added to coffee was among the common adulterants that led to the Pure Food and Drug Act of 1906. I wanted to try chicory not as an adulterant but all on its own.

As I scrubbed my chicory roots, the rootlets came away along with some gritty dirt. I tasted a bit of raw root; it was terribly bitter but at the same time weirdly sweet. Chicory's sweetness comes from inulin, a soluble fiber that feeds "good" bacteria in the gut and is used medicinally to help with constipation and calcium absorption, although it also causes flatulence.

I sliced the six roots and ground them to bits in a small food processor. Then I spread the bits on large pans and put the pans in a convection oven set at 200°F (93°C). Within thirty minutes, the bits were browning. I turned the pans and began turning the chicory bits with a dough scraper every five to ten minutes.

After a little more than an hour and a half of cooking, the chicory was well and evenly browned. As it cooled in the pans, it smelled like caramel. From 3 lb. (1.4 kg) of roots, I had 3 cups of roasted chicory bits.

I put a tablespoon of the chicory bits into a drip coffee maker. Brewed with about 6 ounces (177 mL) of water, the chicory infusion came out just a little lighter than typical American coffee; a darker roast, of course, would have made a darker brew. A darker roast would have also converted more inulin to fructose, which would have made the infusion sweeter. The drink did taste sweet, but not sweet enough to allay its bitterness, and it had none of coffee's aroma. Cream would have improved the brew. Roasted barley might have improved it even more. But after a few sips my husband and I simply abandoned the cup. The stuff was just too bitter.

The next day I tried again, using a tablespoon of chicory bits in a wire basket meant for infusing tea. After two minutes of steeping with water just off the boil, the brew was as dark as most coffee and, again, very bitter. I let the chicory steep for another minute, though, and now the brew was sweeter. I had extracted more inulin (or fructose, or both), and the sweetness helped to balance the bitterness. I was able to drink half the cup. I guessed that brewed chicory might most resemble coffee to people who routinely take their coffee with sugar.

The bitterness of chicory comes from other components, called sesquiterpene lactones (lactucin, lactucopicrin, and 8-deoxylactucin). These substances, like inulin, are extracted by steeping chicory root in water. Although lactucin and its sister chemicals have been little studied, various scientists have found that they discourage insects from feeding on chicory, fight malarial infection in humans, and, in mice, relieve pain and act as a sedative.

The last of these properties—the sedative one—might be a key to chicory's long history as a coffee additive. Not only does roasted chicory root match or exceed coffee in bitterness and balance that bitterness with natural sweetness, but chicory provides a downer drug to counteract the stimulant caffeine.

For several hours after drinking my half cup of chicory brew, I felt sleepy, sluggish, and stupid. I wanted no more to do with chicory coffee.

The jar of roasted chicory root sat on my pantry shelf for years afterward, waiting for someone else to try it. Each year I grew chicory in one form or another, mostly for salads, but my husband and I went on drinking coffee unadulterated. No matter how often I produced chicons, we wouldn't make the roots into a coffee substitute (fortunately, they are good fodder for livestock).

My experiment was unfair to the chicory. For our first tasting, the chicory should have been only 20 percent or so of a coffee-chicory mix, and I should have added milk or cream to our cups. Better yet, I should have replaced my husband and myself as tasters with people who like sweet, milky coffee. And a beignet as accompaniment wouldn't have hurt.

Chicory Coffee

**MAKES ABOUT 1 CUP ROASTED CHICORY
BITS PER POUND OF RAW ROOTS**

**You can either cut the roots into pieces and chop the pieces
to bits in a food processor before roasting, as I did, or slice
the roots thin and grind them after roasting.**

Chicory roots, well scrubbed

1. Either cut the chicory roots into pieces and finely chop them in a food processor, or thinly slice the roots. Spread the pieces on one or more sheet pans.

2. For roasting, I used a convection oven set at 200°F (93°C). In a regular oven, without convection, raise the temperature to 250°F (120°C). (One writer suggests drying sliced chicory root in a food dehydrator before roasting it, which would cut down the roasting time considerably.) Roast the chicory for about 30 minutes, until it is well and uniformly browned. To ensure even browning, check the chicory frequently and turn as needed.

3. If you have roasted slices rather than bits, pulverize the slices in a food processor, blender, or mortar.

4. Combine the ground chicory with ground coffee in the proportion of your choice. Serve the coffee with milk or cream.

The *Many Joys* of Fennel

Probably no plant in my garden is more evocative for me than fennel. A whiff of its aroma or a touch of its soft fronds reminds me of the wild fennel in the field near my house where I grew up, the dry stalks filled with Styrofoam-like "Indian bubble gum." I remember the heavenly, smoky licorice scent after the field burned, as it often did in fall. I remember the wild fennel growing all around Roman ruins in Portugal, each plant bearing not fronds but dozens of little *Theba pisana* snails, estivating—resting in a summer torpor—after having devoured all the foliage. I remember eating a huge platter of those fennel-fed *caracóis* in Lisbon. I remember the *mukhwas*, the bowl of fennel seeds by the cash register in Indian restaurants, some of the seeds candied in pink or white. With the little spoon provided I'd scoop a handful into my palm, sure that there could be no finer digestive and breath freshener. I remember the tidy rows of Florence fennel starts I saw in every home garden in Piemonte, Italy, one late October. I remember the beauty of bronze fennel, the first time I encountered it in a garden in Eugene. And I think of insects, especially wasps, a multitude of species who have no interest in stinging as long as they can gather pollen from the single fennel plant that I let grow beside our deck in Lebanon, Oregon, year after year after year.

Fennel may not have much caloric value, but it certainly has culinary and medicinal worth. From the single plant beside the deck, I snip fronds to sprinkle

over salad or fish or stir into yogurt. I cut stalks to slice thin and use like celery. The stalks are also useful for laying under fish before grilling it, both to perfume the flesh and to keep the skin from sticking to the grill.

When my fennel plant flowers, I mostly leave it to the insects, whose activity my husband and I find mesmerizing. But sometimes I collect the flowers. I first did this after fennel pollen became a fad some years ago. You were supposed to rub fennel pollen over chicken or pork before roasting the meat, dust the pollen over salad or cooked pasta, or use it as a flavoring in bread, cake, or cookies. A chef my daughter worked with even brewed fennel-pollen tea.

I decided to try collecting fennel pollen myself. I pulled a plastic vegetable bag over a blooming fennel head, closed the bag around the stalk, turned the head downward, and shook. After bagging and shaking each flowering head on the plant, I had about a teaspoonful of yellow bits. I spilled them into a dish and let the spiders and other critters crawl away. Looking closely at what remained, I saw little stamens and curled petals. The insects flying around my fennel plant were surely gathering pollen, but any pollen on the dish was invisible to my eye. I concluded that fennel "pollen" was really fennel blossoms.

Another way to gather fennel flowers is to cut blooming flower heads and hang them upside-down in a paper bag. The stamens and petals—and, I suppose, pollen—will fall off in time. The color and flavor of the dry mix will be just a bit less bright than the color and flavor of the fresh flowers, but this may be a more effective method of getting the blossoms to drop.

Fennel flowers make a lovely garnish. To me they are best sprinkled over simply cooked seafood—fish, shrimp, or squid—or even over eggs or buttered toast. You can most appreciate the bright yellow color and honey-sweet, anise-like flavor when the flowers are atop rather than mixed into other food.

Fennel flower heads, left alone, soon turn to seed heads. I try to harvest whole heads while the seeds are still plump and pale. At this stage the seeds are prettiest for kitchen use. If I let them get old and brown, they will be ready for planting, but they risk falling off and planting themselves, and one perennial fennel plant is enough for my garden. Fennel—even the bronze variety—can be quite invasive. I drop the cut heads into a paper bag, where the seeds loosen and fall as they dry.

The seeds have plenty of uses. They are delightful in breads and sausages. They combine well with other spices in curries. They can be eaten in mukhwas, raw or roasted, on their own or combined with seeds such as sesame, dill, and flax. When bruised in a mortar, fennel seeds make a tasty herbal tea. The tea is supposed to ameliorate digestive problems in adults and colic in babies. Nursing mothers sometimes drink fennel tea to increase their milk supply, although some researchers suggest that anethole—the main constituent of the aromatic oils in anise, star-anise, and fennel—may be toxic in babies who take in too much. Anethole is estrogenic, so fennel tea may possibly ease post-menopausal complaints. I drink fennel tea because it tastes good.

Sometimes fennel is grown as a vegetable. This is Florence fennel, the kind sold in stores as anise (which it isn't) or *finocchio* (Italian for "fennel," but Italians clarify matters by calling common fennel *finocchietto*). Common and Florence fennel are the same species, *Foeniculum vulgare*, but Florence fennel is a special variety, *F. vulgare* var. *azoricum*. Although the name indicates that the variety came from the Azores, it is most celebrated in Italy. The differences between the two fennels become obvious after several weeks' growth: Whereas my common fennel plant soars to more than 6 ft. (1.8 m) every summer, Florence fennel develops a thick, bulbous lower stem and reaches only about 2 ft. (60 cm).

I will never forget the fennel salad I had at a café in Italy. It was a heap of thinly sliced fennel bulb combined with some orange segments, dressed with oil and vinegar and salt, and topped with slices of hard, salty cheese, probably Pecorino Romano. With bread on the side, that salad made a very satisfying meal.

Since then I've often made a similar salad. Because fennel slices can be tough, I slice them very thin with a mandoline. Then I salt them and let them rest for at least fifteen minutes to soften. I pour off any accumulated liquid before adding dressing and other ingredients.

Florence fennel makes delicious soup, too. I cook the sliced bulb with potatoes and chicken stock and then purée the mixture with sour cream. Added fennel fronds can heighten the fennel flavor and serve as a pretty garnish as well.

Florence fennel is a somewhat difficult plant to grow well. Getting good bulbous stems depends on mild weather, fertile soil, and plentiful water. You can plant fennel in early spring or, for fall harvest, in mid-summer. In either season, though, erratic weather can foil your efforts. Heat and drought tend to keep the stems from bulbing.

I learned the Italian trick of growing good finocchio by observing Piemonte gardens: Ignore the assertions that fennel must be sown directly in the garden. Instead, start the seeds in pots indoors, beginning in February. Don't be afraid of crowding the little plants; they won't mind. When they are big enough to

transplant, you can space them out. If the weather cooperates, you can end up with uniform fennel plants in neat rows, all of them soon forming bulbs.

All fennel is perennial, so if you leave the roots of your Florence fennel in the ground after harvest, more heads may form—but they will be small, like second-growth cabbage heads. For this reason, Florence fennel is normally grown as an annual.

Also like cabbage, fennel bulbs have a solid core. If you use the bulbs when they are relatively young and small, you can slice the core along with the outer layers. One fall, though, I was so late in harvesting two fennel bulbs that they became huge, and frozen solid. I cooked the outer layers into a puréed soup, and then, unwilling to throw out the cores, invented—or re-invented—something truly unusual.

I had been reading Tim Richardson's *Sweets*, a wonderfully entertaining history of candy. Tim had made me think how medieval my *Joy of Jams* was. All those fruit pastes and syrups started with recipes the Arabs developed or borrowed from the Persians. These treats became popular throughout Europe in the Middle Ages. My book even includes some recipes for crystallized fruits, which are simply preserves with the syrup drained off. To a large extent, *The Joy of Jams* is about medieval confectionery.

But I'd left out candied vegetables. "All kinds of roots and stalks were being candied in England by the sixteenth century," according to Tim. They included parsley roots, angelica stalks, lettuce stalks, and stranger foods like sea holly, borage, and bugloss. They also included fennel roots.

My fennel had tough, rough, dirty roots, and I didn't want to waste my time on them. But the cores seemed to hold some promise. So, I candied them, much as you would candy cherries or citrus peels or pineapple.

The finished candies ranged in color from pale gold to amber. They were firm but not tough and had a mild but appealing fennel flavor. If you wanted to intensify the flavor, you could add a few fennel seeds to the syrup.

I thought about including the candied fennel cubes on a Christmas dessert platter, alongside my candied Asian pears, or in a Christmas pudding, but I didn't hide them away fast enough. They got eaten almost immediately. I must admit that I got my share.

Candied Fennel Cores

MAKES ABOUT 1 CUP

Although this is a simple recipe, you must allow a full day for the cooking and resting steps and at least several hours for the drying.

5 ounces (140 g) Florence fennel cores, cut into ⅜ in. (1 cm) cubes

⅔ cup (158 mL) water, plus more for cooking the fennel

⅔ cup (135 g) sugar

Pinch of cream of tartar

1. Put the fennel cubes into a saucepan with enough water to cover them. Simmer them until they are tender when pierced with a fork, about 20 minutes. Drain the fennel, and set it aside.

2. Combine the water, sugar, and cream of tartar in a saucepan, and heat the mixture gently until the sugar dissolves. Bring the syrup to a boil and continue boiling until it is reduced by almost a quarter, to thicken the syrup slightly. Add the fennel and bring the mixture back to a full boil. Once it reaches a boil, remove the pan from the heat. Let the mixture cool, and then cover the pan and let it stand at room temperature for 8 to 12 hours.

3. Return the pan to the stove. Simmer the fennel in the syrup until the cubes are partially translucent and the syrup reaches thread stage (230°F or 110°C), about 25 minutes. Remove the pan from the heat, and let the mixture cool. Let the fennel cubes rest in the syrup, covered, at room temperature for 8 to 12 hours.

4. Drain the fennel cubes. Set them to dry in a warm place until they are no longer sticky. I used a food dehydrator, but you could instead put them in an oven set at a very low heat or even on top of a woodstove.

5. Store the fennel cubes in an airtight container.

Tasting Lavender

At a potluck one year I was eager to taste the lavender lemonade, something I'd never made myself and drunk only once or twice before. But the drink was sweetened to a child's taste; I guessed it had been made with twice the volume of sugar as lemon juice, *before* the lavender syrup was added. And because the lemonade was already so sweet, apparently, only a little lavender syrup was included, so little that I could barely taste the lavender.

It occurred to me that the culinary use of lavender was a growing trend that I'd mostly ignored. I had used lavender for repelling moths in closets and dresser drawers, and I'd stirred the flowers into blackberry jam for a mysterious resinous touch, but the smell of lavender never made me hungry. I liked looking at my hardy, tidy, deer- and drought-resistant lavender plants more than I liked sniffing them.

Lavender has traditionally been little used for cooking. The name of this herb, after all, comes from a Latin word for washing, and lavender is still most beloved as a scent for soap. Although southern France is famous for its lavender production, most of the oil is used in perfumery. The famous *herbes de Provence*, typically rubbed on meats for grilling, sometimes include lavender blossoms, but lavender has no place in the certified *label rouge* mix, which comprises only thyme, rosemary, savory, oregano, and basil. French cooks do sometimes infuse lavender flowers in milk to flavor ice cream or custard, and the flowers are occasionally used in tisanes and in vinegar or vinaigrette, but other culinary uses seem rare in France.

Americans, in contrast, have been experimenting freely with lavender in foods. I've eaten both lavender meringues and lavender shortbread. A candy-maker produces caramel sauce and caramel candies from cream infused with lavender. Owners of a lavender farm recommend using lavender stems as skewers for fruit or shrimp kabobs; freezing the blossoms in ice cubes; infusing honey and jams with the flowers; adding lavender sprigs to pink champagne cocktails, lemonade, or punch; and sprinkling the flowers over salads, fruit, and desserts. Renee Shepherd, of Renee's Garden Seeds, puts lavender sugar in hot or iced tea; makes a syrup with lavender, dessert wine, and orange juice to pour over cut fresh fruit; rubs lavender blossoms in lemon juice and olive oil on pork or lamb for grilling; and tosses lavender stems, leaves, or flowers over the hot coals while grilling lamb, pork, or salmon. American bartenders, likewise, have been making their own lavender syrup and adding it to cocktails.

If I wanted to experiment with fresh lavender that year, I knew, I had to hurry. The flowers are best harvested while still in bud, and mine were beginning to open. The day after the potluck dawned sunny and dry, so in the cool of the morning I sniffed my various specimens of *Lavandula angustifolia*—"narrow-leafed" lavender, true lavender, or English lavender.

In case you're choosing lavender to plant or trying to identify lavender plants already in your garden, here's a quick introduction. Aside from their half-hardiness and their need for excellent drainage, lavender plants are easy to grow. They not only resist both drought and deer, but they need no fertilizer. "English" lavender, like other lavender species, is native not to England but to southern Europe. Still, it is hardy enough to grow in England and other cool places. It grows in 2 to 3 ft. (60 to 90 cm) sweetly scented mounds.

Toothy-leafed "French" lavender (*Lavandula dentata*) lacks cold-tolerance; for me it has survived no more than a few years without protection. "Spanish" lavender (*L. stoechas*) has fat flower heads that are each amusingly topped with four large violet-pink bracts. *L. stoechas* is hardier than *L. dentata*, but winters

that are very cold and wet can destroy it. In any case, *L. stoechas* and *L. dentata* have fragrances too bitter and camphor-like to use in cooking, as does the powerfully aromatic *L. latifolia*, also known as spike lavender.

Yet another kind of lavender is *lavandin*, or *Lavandula ×intermedia*, a cross of *L. angustifolia* and *L. latifolia*. Lavandin cultivars are just a little less hardy than *L. angustifolia*. They usually grow tall, to about 3 ft. (1 m), and their flower spikes can be 12 in. (30 cm) long. Because of their high production of both flower spikes and essential oil, lavandins are now the most cultivated lavenders in Provence. Many people believe they are better in perfume than in food, but others disagree. Renee Shepherd recommends *L. ×intermedia* 'Provence' for the kitchen.

For my lemonade, I used the intensely fragrant, deepest blue flowers of 'Sharon Roberts', a *Lavandula angustifolia* cultivar introduced by Nichols Garden Nursery. I wanted to make lemonade that tasted more of lavender than sugar. But how should I instill the lavender aroma? I could flavor the sugar, as Renee Shepherd suggests, by burying several lavender spikes in a jar of sugar and closing the jar for a week. Or I could make up a batch of plain lemonade, add lavender flowers or spikes, and chill the lemonade until the flavor seemed right. Alternatively, I could make a batch of lavender syrup, which I could keep on hand for making lemonade or cocktails by the glass, with the lavender syrup standing in for sugar (in the case of lemonade) or plain syrup (in the case of cocktails). I chose the syrup option.

I decided to follow the typical sugar-water ratio for a bartender's simple syrup: 1 part sugar to 1 part water. A 1:1 syrup needs refrigeration or pasteurization for long keeping, but it won't tend to crystallize, as a 2:1 syrup will. And I would use plenty of lavender, more than was called for in any recipe I could find.

My syrup turned out nearly colorless, with a silvery tinge, a strong floral aroma, and a mildly bitter taste. Even without alcohol, I knew, it would make a grown-up lemonade.

Lavender Syrup

MAKES ABOUT 2 ¼ CUPS (530 mL)

When I sent my son Ben home with a jar of this syrup, he said he would try it various cocktails, such as a Lavender Aviation, with the syrup replacing the *crème de violette* used in the standard Aviation.

2 cups (473 mL) water
2 cups (400 g) sugar
6 tablespoons fresh lavender buds

1. Bring the ingredients slowly to a boil, stirring to dissolve the sugar. Remove the pan from the heat and cover it.

2. After 30 minutes, strain the syrup through a fine-mesh strainer. Press the flowers in the strainer to extract as much syrup as possible.

Lavender Lemonade, *by the* Glass

Put the ice cubes into a 12-ounce (350 mL) glass. Pour the lemon juice and lavender syrup over the ice. Add the club soda and stir.

SERVES 1

This lemonade is more aromatic than sweet, and slightly, refreshingly bitter. Ben suggested adding gin to the lemonade. For me, club soda makes this drink celebratory enough, and with plain water it's a fine accompaniment to meals.

About 6 ice cubes

1 tablespoon fresh lemon juice

1 tablespoon lavender syrup

¾ cup (175 mL) club soda or water

Scarlet Runners *for* Winter Meals

I was filling baskets with skinny French beans and Spanish flat beans one summer when I noticed that some of my scarlet runner beans were ready to eat. Why in the world had I planted so many beans?

I was growing runners for the first time in at least seven years. I'd stopped planting them when my children had stopped asking me to erect bean tepees, which had never seemed worth the trouble of building. For years I had imagined the kids sitting inside a lovely live, green tepee on a hot summer day, making fairy houses or reading a picture book, and they apparently shared this fantasy. But it rarely came true. Hoeing in the tepee was difficult, so before long the space would fill with tall weeds. Watering was always troublesome, too. I would wrap a soaker hose around the perimeter of the tepee, but the hose would leak, from a tear or from a faulty connection, and form a mud puddle. And then one day the wind would come up and bend the tepee to one side, and, despite my efforts at straightening, the tepee would lean ridiculously for the rest of the summer. Unless I let it collapse altogether, picking the highest bean pods was nearly impossible; a ladder wouldn't fit inside the tepee, and when I set the ladder on the outside the peak of the tepee was too far away to reach.

But eventually I realized that I missed the scarlet runner bean's bright red flowers and meaty pods. I thought of an easier trellising system: I would anchor a cattle panel with metal fence stakes and then tie tall bamboo poles to the cattle panel. Our bamboo grew to only about 15 ft. (4.6 m), and runner vines can run longer, but I figured they could hang from the top, dangling their pods to within my reach. In early summer I planted a small handful of scarlet runner beans and set up my sturdy new trellis. (In recent years my favorite trellis for runner beans has been a 16 ft., or 4.9 m, cattle panel arched and staked between two raised beds set 4 ft., or 1.2 m, apart.)

Now the first meaty pods had to be picked, or else they would get tough and fibrous. At that moment, though, I had no appetite for them. They were too few to bother blanching and freezing, and the kitchen refrigerator was stuffed full of other vegetables. Could I do as so many other gardeners did—enjoy the flowers and let the beans go? I was too frugal for that.

There was an obvious alternative: I could leave the pods alone now and shell them later. I had always saved shelled runner beans for later planting, but only a handful or two, and only at the end of the season. I'd never thought to save the whole crop for drying and eating.

Growing your own beans for drying takes dedication, especially in the Pacific Northwest. You've got to put the seeds in the ground early enough for the pods to fill and start drying before the fall rains begin to rot them. Rotting is especially likely with bush beans, which often rest their pods directly on the wet ground. And, assuming you can collect enough full, healthy pods, you might need an hour to shell enough little beans by hand for one family dinner.

But runner beans are more amenable to drying than bush beans or any common beans. When provided with a trellis, runner beans hang their pods high, where they're less prone to rot. The plants can survive a few light frosts. And because the seeds are big, about 1 in. (2.5 cm) or longer, shelling goes fast.

Thanks to a dry September and a fairly warm October (during which the plants did indeed withstand light frosts), I was able to put off harvesting the runner beans until after Halloween. Then I tossed the pods, in various stages of drying, into a tray in the greenhouse. In mid-November I shelled some. With ten minutes' work I had a pound. The shelled beans were beautiful, violet speckled with black.

To fully appreciate the beans as food, I decided to serve them plain. I soaked and boiled them (they took somewhat longer to cook than most common

beans, because the skins of runner beans are rather thick). Then I puréed them with a little olive oil, salt, and smoked paprika. With fresh, warm homemade tortillas, this was lunch. The bean purée was grayer than refried pinto beans but delicious, with a smooth, creamy texture and a mild flavor lacking in some beany element that, I realized, I really don't like.

What *was* this unbean-like bean? I wanted to know its place in botany, history, and cookery.

Botanists, I learned, call runner beans *Phaseolus coccineus*. The species name refers to the color of the blossoms—red, like cochineal—although in some varieties the blossoms are white. Unlike *P. vulgaris*—common kidney beans—runner beans are perennial, though outside of the tropics we can grow them only as annuals. In the highlands of southern Mexico and Central America, where the beans originated, the seeds come in many colors—white, pink, purple, and black—and go by *frijoles botil*, *ayocotl*, or *ayocote* (note the similarity of the last two words to the French *haricot*). The starchy roots get so big in Mesoamerica that they too are traditionally used as food—as a textural addition to *pulque*, for example—though my roots looked too scrawny to bother with.

Many American gardeners love the scarlet runner primarily as a hummingbird attractant, yet this variety was developed by the hummingbird-less English, who at first used the flowers in bouquets. John Tradescant the Younger, a botanist who traveled to Virginia between 1628 and 1637, gets credit for introducing the bean to England. I doubt he found it in Virginia at such an early date, although Thomas Jefferson probably grew it much later at Monticello; the French name *haricot d'Espagne* suggests a more likely path of transmission. More than a century after the scarlet runner came to England, Philip Miller, through his *Gardeners Dictionary*, popularized it as food—"the best sort for the table"—although he didn't make clear whether he liked the bean green or shelled. In any case, when the English eat runner beans today, they are nearly always in the pod.

Phaseolus coccineus is popular in Spain as a dried bean, but usually in a form with white seeds. In Spain you can buy packages of big white runner beans labeled as *el judión de La Granja* or *judión de El Barco* for your *olla*.

Mexican and Central American farmers grow runner beans less than they used to, since the vines don't fit well with modern monoculture. And these farmers don't grow scarlet runners at all, at least not on a commercial scale.

But Mexico and Central America still have their own favorite runner-bean varieties. Best known are *ayocote morado*, with pale lavender flowers and purple seeds, and *ayocote negro*, with big orange-red flowers and seeds that dry purple-black. These varieties are available for gardeners from various little seed companies that advertise on the Internet. Some companies are also selling them for eating—for a price, at this writing, of $7.50 to $11.00 a pound.

If Americans are paying this much for imported purple and black runner beans, why aren't we eating the speckled ones from our gardens? All runner beans, says the website of the main purveyor, Rancho Gordo, "are great with loads of garlic and wild mushrooms or just as part of a mixed salad. In Mexico, you find them served with a chile sauce or in a soup, but in Europe, you might see them drowned in good fruity olive oil and a squeeze of lemon juice before dusting with sea salt." Isn't that inspiring?

In December I shelled some more of my runner beans and stewed them with tomatoes. I loved how the beans stayed intact and took on a handsome deep red color, somewhere between brick and burgundy.

As I later learned, runners make good, fresh shell beans as well as dry beans. Recently I picked some green pods, bulging with their seeds, after several days of rainfall and a heavy frost. Green pods are harder to open than dry ones, but I shelled the beans with little trouble by bending each green pod in half, usually in the direction of the little curl at the end, until the pod split at the seam. The seeds showed no sign of frost damage or mold. They were at various stages of maturity, with some still small and pale pink, but that was no problem. I just simmered them together until they were all tender.

Scarlet runner beans for planting are easy to find. A favorite cultivar is 'Scarlet Emperor', selected for its long, tasty pods. Some cultivars are classed with scarlet runners even though they lack the all-scarlet flowers. Two of these are 'Painted Lady', with bi-colored red and white blossoms, and 'Sunset', with salmon-pink flowers.

Stewed Runner Beans *with* Tomatoes

SERVES ABOUT 6

Although this dish without alteration will especially please vegetarians, it is also excellent with cooked bacon or sausage slices added toward the end of cooking. You can of course vary the seasonings; try adding oregano, cumin, or bay.

About 2 cups (12 oz. or 340 g) dried scarlet runner beans, soaked overnight or not

Sprig of sage

5 garlic cloves, divided

2 tablespoons olive oil

1 large onion (about 8 oz. or 227 g), cut into wedges

½ cup diced red peppers, sweet or mildly hot

4 cups (946 mL) canned tomatoes, with their juice

3 fennel seeds

2 pinches of ground saffron

½ cup chopped parsley

Freshly ground black pepper

Salt

Bread or cooked rice, for serving

1. Put the beans, sage, and a single garlic clove into a pot. Add plenty of water, and set the pot over medium heat. Bring the water to a boil, and then lower the heat. Simmer the beans until they are tender, which will take 1 to 2 hours.

2. Put the oil into a large skillet set over medium heat. Add the onions, and sauté them until they are tender. Crush the 4 remaining garlic cloves, and add them to the skillet along with the peppers. Sauté the vegetables until the garlic releases its fragrance. Add the tomatoes, fennel, saffron, and parsley, and twist the pepper mill over the pan 2 or 3 times. Break up the tomatoes with a spoon or spatula. When the mixture is hot, add the beans. Boil the mixture until it's suitably thick, about 10 minutes. Add salt to taste, and serve with bread or rice.

Sweet Parsnips

I first made parsnip soup many years ago, after listening with my then-small eldest child to Peggy Seeger sing, "What Did You Have for Your Supper?" on the record *American Folk Songs for Children*. I didn't read the song's title in the record notes, though, and I heard the words as *"What'll* you have for your supper?"

What'll you have for your supper,
Jimmy Randall, my son?
What'll you have for your supper,
My own little one?
Sweet milk and sweet parsnips;
Mother make my bed soon,
Because I'm tired at the heart
And I want to lie down.

With each *sweet*, Peggy's voice soared to the top of the octave; Jimmy was pleading for sweet white comfort food that Mother and no other could provide. Or so I thought.

Little did I know that I was hearing a surviving fragment of "Lord Randall," an Anglo-Scottish ballad about a man who may have lived in the thirteenth century or thereabouts, until he was poisoned—by his sweetheart at dinner, according to most versions of the song. In typical versions she also poisons Randall's dogs, who "swell up." Feeling poorly after the meal, Randall goes

home to his mother. The story is told through conversation between mother and son as poor Randall heads for his deathbed. Fuller versions don't mention milk or parsnips; usually he has eaten eels or other fish. And Mother is always less curious about the tainted food than she is about the distribution of Randall's worldly goods.

The parsnip has been popular since Roman times, though it was probably thin and woody and suitable only for flavoring until about the time Lord Randall was getting sick on eels. Then gardeners developed it into a fleshy, aromatic root that at its best cooks up quite tender. The modern English name *parsnip* may have been influenced by *parsley*, for a white-rooted cousin, and *turnip*, for an unrelated and fleshier root vegetable. The parsnip is more like the carrot than either of these, but sweeter and starchier, with less bitterness. Some people describe the parsnip's flavor as "nutty." They are probably thinking of chestnuts.

At a book club meeting, in the middle of a discussion of race and gender in nineteenth-century America and the founding of the U.S. Geological Survey, somebody asked the inevitable sort of question: How do you grow parsnips? (Our husbands think we talk about *them* at these meetings. We do, sometimes. But more often the talk turns to gardening.)

I felt an immediate surge of affection for the new member who asked about parsnips. Parsnip lovers are rarities, it seems. Why is this? Who can dislike that carroty flavor combined with extra sweetness? It's true that parsnips themselves are a little bitter, but their natural sugars, as well as fat added in cooking, tend to hide the bitterness. Is the parsnip just too blandly white next to the sunny orange carrot? Or is the parsnip so pricey in the market that most people never even try it?

Why such a humble root should cost so much is puzzling, but at least I could take a stab at the new member's question. For my best parsnip crops I must thank my friend Lisa, who told me to toss the seeds onto bare soil in February. This works because parsnip seeds require constant moisture for about two weeks while they think about sprouting. Here in the Willamette Valley, we generally have that constant moisture in February. Our frosts continue until mid-May, but that matters not at all to the hardy parsnip.

Most gardeners know that you're supposed to leave your parsnips in the ground until after the first frost to sweeten them up. This is what I've done, though I might like a less-sweet parsnip, too. I usually leave most of my roots in the ground for much longer still. A virtue of parsnips is that you can store

them right where they have grown all through the winter—unless the water table rises into their root zone, which causes them to rot, or unless the weather is so brutally cold that a mound of mulch won't keep them from freezing.

But when you plant parsnips in February for digging in late fall and winter, you're at least doubling the usual four-month growing period. And when parsnips grow for that long they develop two problems: They get so big that they become hard to dig, and they develop a hard core that gets bigger and tougher over time. My fall- and winter-dug parsnips have averaged 8 in. (20 cm) across and 18 in. (46 cm) long. By mid-winter they may have as much core as tender flesh, which makes for much effort in the kitchen and a big pile of trimmings. And if left undug until late winter the plants sprout new top growth, because, like their carrot cousins, they are biennial. As parsnips prepare to produce seeds, their roots become tough and inedible.

Some parsnip varieties may be more prone to tough cores than others. 'Tender and True' is described as "almost coreless," and 'Harris Early Model' is said to have no core at all. If you have a high water table in winter, maybe one of the short- and thick-rooted German varieties would be an even better alternative. But I have grown various parsnip varieties and found little difference among them.

So, here's how I tentatively advised the book club to go about growing parsnips: Plant seeds in late spring, around the time of the last frost. Use seeds harvested the previous fall (and don't buy seeds that have sat in a rack in a warm building for months), because old parsnip seeds won't sprout. Keep the seeds moist for two to three weeks, until they germinate. Don't give parsnips too much nitrogen-rich fertilizer; it's said to make their roots hairy. Let them grow for 105 to 130 days, depending on the variety, to maturity. Start digging them as soon thereafter as you like. If you have time to devise some out-of-ground storage system, such as a clamp or box of sand, dig them all soon after the first autumn frost.

I'll stand by that advice now, except for the part about the late-spring planting. Since I've begun planting later, I've had few homegrown parsnips. I've tried covering the seeds with a board for a time and even germinating the seeds on damp paper towels, with little luck. In some places, such as the American Midwest and New Zealand, parsnips escape the garden and grow wild in nearby pastures, where their tops, containing photoactive chemicals called furanocoumarins, sometimes cause sunburn in horses and blister

sheep's tongues (they are also said to cause severe skin rashes on some humans, so wear gloves when handling the greens, or at least wash your hands afterward). Lisa tells me that her parsnips have gone feral, too, though they haven't escaped the garden. But my parsnips have never attempted to naturalize, even though I usually let some plants go to seed.

I'm going back to planting in February. The more parsnips the better, I figure, even if they're oversize.

Whether they have been stored in a cellar or left in the ground, parsnips are a comfort on a cold night in winter or early spring when you're craving something sweet, starchy, and soothing. Preparing parsnips for the table is easy when you don't have big, tough cores to cut out. Betty Fussell, in *I Hear America Cooking*, recommends boiling the roots, dousing them in cold water, and then slipping off their skins, but in my experience parsnips have no more in the way of skins than carrots, which I rarely peel at all. If I'm having trouble scrubbing my parsnips completely clean, though, I peel them with a swivel peeler. Then I use them in most of the ways you might use carrots. Parsnips are good roasted, on their own or along with carrots or chunks of squash or wedges of sweet potato, or fried, in sticks or as chips. You might purée your parsnips with apples or carrots or potatoes, serve them diced in a chicken pot pie, and flavor them with curry powder, ginger, or nutmeg. You can fill ravioli with puréed parsnips or combine the purée with flour in gnocchi. You can even use parsnips like pumpkin in a custard pie (a recipe from New Zealand includes another comforting ingredient, a cup of whiskey). But my favorite, as you may guess, is soup.

Parsnip Soup

SERVES ABOUT 2

When I first heard Peggy Seeger's song, I knew just what I wanted to make with parsnips—and it's what I most like to make with them today: a puréed soup with sweet milk. By the way, I don't believe Jimmy Randall ever got sick on sweet milk and parsnips. It was his mother who fed him the soup, I'm sure, and he woke up the next morning feeling fit and lively. Even his dogs survived. At least that's how I like to sing the song.

1 medium onion (about 6 oz. or 170 g), diced

2 tablespoons butter

2 small or 1 large parsnip (about 10 oz. or 283 g), diced

4 cups (948 mL) chicken stock

½ cup (113 mL) milk, cream, or half-and-half

Salt

White pepper

Grated nutmeg

1. Put the onion and butter in a pot set over medium heat, and sauté until the onion is soft, about 10 minutes. Add the parsnips and the chicken stock, and bring the mixture to a simmer. Simmer the parsnips in the stock until they are tender, about 10 minutes. Stir in the milk. Season with salt, white pepper, and nutmeg to taste. Let the mixture cool for 5 minutes, and then purée it in a blender.

2. Reheat the soup before serving, if needed. If you like, top each bowl with another grating of nutmeg.

Poppies *for* Seed

I was visiting Oregon State University one day when I came upon a big bed of opium poppies, next to the sidewalk on a main road through campus. How curious, I thought. The university has superb landscaping, but it is mostly made up of trees, shrubs, and lawn; I wasn't used to seeing big beds of annuals here. And wasn't growing opium a risky thing to do amid more than thirty thousand playful young adults?

No matter. The poppies were exactly like the ones I'd grown throughout our six years in the Santa Cruz Mountains of California. The big petals were hot pink, with short strokes of purple extending from the center of each flower. The pods were oval, and beneath the edge of the little flat cap, on the drier pods, was a series of small holes, from which the little black seeds would scatter when the wind blew. Some of the pods were dry enough to harvest. I pulled one off and put it in my pocket, taking care not to spill the seeds in the transfer. At home I would scrape the fresh seeds from my pocket, shake more from the pod, and store the seeds for sowing in the fall. Every year thereafter I would have a delightful show of pink poppies behind the farmhouse.

Each autumn I would cut the stems and pack them pod-down into grocery bags. When I was sure the pods were completely dry, I'd shake the bags until the pods had spilled their seeds. I would put a fraction of the seeds aside to plant or give away, and I'd store the rest in an airtight container in the freezer, where they could keep for years without going rancid. I sprinkled those seeds over almost every loaf of bread I baked.

Opium poppies, of course, are not just food; they have for thousands of years served as one of humanity's most valuable medicines, especially in treating diarrhea and pain. But only once did I consider using the poppies as a drug. Finding myself in agonizing pain one day, I went hunting for one of the bottles of little pills that had come home with my children after their wisdom-teeth extractions. But I couldn't find the pills. And then it occurred to me that I had green poppy pods in the garden, at just the right stage for extracting opium.

Standing in front of the sunny bed behind the garage, I slit a pod vertically with a sharp knife. The milky white opium began oozing out immediately. I watched it accumulate, and then I touched my tongue to it. I shrieked and spat. And spat and spat and spat. Opium was the bitterest thing I had ever tasted. It must take true desperation to be an opium eater. I decided I was not so desperate after all. I would endure my pain.

When we moved into Lebanon, a former mill town with conspicuous drug problems, I wasn't sure about growing poppies. I needed the backyard for vegetables and the front yard for fruits, so the poppies could go only into the long planting strip lining the street. I tossed some seeds there. They sprouted and the plants grew and blossomed, the bees tumbled joyfully in the pollen, and no one complained.

In late summer, though, just after I'd cut down all the poppy stalks, I saw through the window a scraggly-haired, scraggly-bearded old man standing on the sidewalk and staring at the spot where the opium poppies used to be. He came to the door and knocked. He wondered about the flowers that had been there, he said. He had a friend who needed such flowers. This friend had a serious medical condition and wanted flowers of that sort as treatment for it. The friend ate the leaves as medicine! The man looked startled at the brilliance of his own final lie.

I gave the man some seeds. Everyone should have a right to grow his own medicine, I figured. But I resolved not to plant poppies in the front yard again. I would make room in the backyard.

Now I considered searching for a different poppy cultivar. With such a small garden, I was choosing plants more carefully than I'd done on the farm. If I was going to use precious backyard space for poppies, couldn't I find a cultivar with the big, blue-gray, sweet seeds of the commercial trade? Those seeds were hard to find in grocery stores, and when I did find them they were

often rancid. I figured I should really be producing my own. (Grocers, by the way, should store poppy seeds in freezers, where they will keep well for years.)

I imagined I would have many varieties to choose from. People have been using and breeding *Papaver somniferum*, the "sleep-inducing" opium poppy, for thousands of years, since the early Neolithic age. The plant apparently originated in the Mediterranean region and traveled eastward on the Silk Road, taking root wherever dry summers allowed it to mature without rotting. Besides needing rain at germination and dry weather at maturation, the poppy was very adaptable. It tolerated drought and sandy and alkaline soils. You could sow the seeds in fall, and the plants would grow slowly over the winter. If the winter was too cold, you could sow the seeds in early spring instead. If you let the seed stalks stand long enough for the plants to self-sow, you might in summer find both bigger, earlier-blooming plants that had begun growing in fall and later-blooming plants that had sprouted in the spring. Or you might find only one or the other, depending on how the weather had been. The plant hedged its bets. As it spread to Central and Eastern Europe, to the Middle East and on to Afghanistan and all the way to Southeast Asia, the poppy adapted to local conditions, and people saved seeds of their strongest plants.

The world has ended up with at least eleven hundred opium poppy varieties. The flowers come in white, pale lavender, pink, red, purple, and orange, and they are often variegated. There is even a stunningly sky blue variety, from the Himalayas. Opium poppy seeds are white, yellow, brown, black, gray, blue, or mauve. White or pale flowers usually give white or pale seeds, and flowers of purple or another strong color usually give blue, gray, or black seeds, but the association of petal color and seed color isn't absolute. The pods can be spherical, squat, oblong, egg-shaped, and even pear-shaped. Most varieties grow no more than 3 ft. (1 m) tall, but one cultivar, 'Giganteum', is said to grow to 5 ft. (1.5 m) and produce pods as big as golf balls.

Poppy breeding has taken divergent directions. The newest varieties are the ornamentals, which may have doubled blossoms, astonishing colors, and ragged petal edges. 'Black Swan' is ragged and doubled; 'Danish Flag' is red and ragged with white centers; and 'Lilac Pompom' truly looks like a pink pompom. These varieties may have small pods and seeds too small to bother eating.

Beyond the ornamentals, a main difference among poppy varieties is the presence or absence of vents on the pods. Poppies with these little holes, such as my pink poppies, are more like their wild ancestor. You save the seeds simply by placing the stalks upside-down in a bag, shaking the bag, and letting the seeds fall out.

Both seed producers and opium producers believe that closed-pod varieties are superior. But these pods make seed saving more difficult; you must thresh the pods (put them in a sack and stamp on them) and then sieve out the seeds. An advantage is that you don't risk losing seeds when the wind blows. You also have more control over where your poppies will grow the following year, though you must remember to sow them, and to do so at the right time. Sowing seeds in the greenhouse and transplanting the seedlings will not work, because poppies have taproots. You may need to stratify the seeds—chill them for two to four weeks—to ensure that they will germinate. Especially if you have only a few plants, you may not be able to rely on nature to produce your seeds for you. (Actually, although the closed-pod trait is dominant, nowhere have the vents gone away entirely. Even meticulous growers of seed poppies expect a quarter of their plants to have vents. And some plants will bear both vented and closed pods.)

Another big difference among poppy varieties is the alkaloid content. Alkaloids such as morphine, codeine, and thebaine are what make opium both bitter and medically effective. Despite the bitterness of my pink poppy's exudation, vented-pod varieties are said to be relatively low in alkaloids. These varieties are uncommon in Asia. This suggests to me that poppies were first bred, in Europe, for their seeds, and that some of the closed-pod varieties carried eastward have since been bred for higher opium content. Since the 1970s, however, European varieties with blue-gray seeds and closed pods have been bred for very low alkaloid content. European governments strictly regulate the alkaloid content of poppies grown within their borders. In the Czech Republic, the maximum alkaloid content of dry poppy pods is 0.8 percent, and the usual content is lower, 0.3 to 0.7 percent. Still, these amounts are high enough that the poppy "straw"—the crushed pods and the tops of the stalks—is carried to a factory for the extraction of morphine, the most abundant of the opium alkaloids.

None of the literature I've perused about opium poppies has mentioned seed size, but the commercial blue poppy seeds are substantially bigger than the little black seeds from my vented pink poppies. I suspect that the bigger seeds are easier to grind, and I suspect, too, that the seeds *must* be ground to provide much nourishment for humans. Europeans make special mills

just for grinding poppy seeds, whose oil would gum up grain mills. I have found an alternative way to process poppy seeds, as you'll see in the recipe for Mohnzelten, but I might buy a little mill someday just to see if it grinds my tiny black poppy seeds or lets them slip through whole.

The big blue-gray poppy seeds I wanted to buy are often labeled as "breadseed" poppy seeds (a seed company must have devised this moniker to mislead the Drug Enforcement Administration). I was surprised to find only a few varieties listed by U.S. seed merchants. I chose a type, finally, from the village of Ziar, Slovakia. With petals that were pale lavender, almost white, and faded purple centers, the poppy clearly hadn't been bred for looks. But it had closed pods and big blue-gray seeds. That it didn't self-sow was unfortunate, because I had trouble getting it to germinate the following year. Still, the seeds I collected were big and sweet-tasting.

I've since found that poppy-seed paste made from blue and black seeds turns out approximately the same color, and that no difference in sweetness is detectable when the same small amount of sugar or honey is added to the blue-seed paste and the black-seed paste. For bread and pastry fillings, then, my black poppy seeds are as good as the blue.

But perhaps white poppy seeds taste a little different. To find out, I'm trying at this writing to start a white-seeded variety called 'Elka'. It too comes from Slovakia. I don't know what Slovaks do with white poppies, but Indians like them for thickening savory dishes.

Assuming that poppy seeds are well ground, they are very nourishing. They contain about 47 percent fat, about 23 percent protein, and substantial amounts of vitamin E, calcium, magnesium, zinc, iron, and manganese. Throughout central and eastern Europe, they are relished in cakes, breads, and pastries. Nowhere, however, are poppy seeds a major part of the human diet. The Czechs are probably the biggest consumers, and they eat only about a pound per person per year.

Over the centuries, the peasants who have relied on poppies—always smallholders on poor land—have done much more with the plants than extract the opium and eat the seeds. They have eaten the young leaves as greens—not as medicine but as a vegetable (before the pods form, the leaves are free of alkaloids). They have pressed the seeds to produce a sweet, nutty oil, useful for both cooking and lighting. They have sold some of the oil for use in paints, varnishes, perfumes, drugs, and soaps. They have mixed the pressed seeds with wheat flour to make a coarse but protein-rich bread. They have fed the press cake, stems, and leaves to their cattle, and used the poppy straw as stable bedding. When tired, aching, or sick, these farmers have made a soothing bitter tea from the crumbled dry poppy pods. They have built their economies and their lives around poppies.

No wonder U.S. attitudes about opium poppies seem ludicrous to traditional growers, such as those in Turkey, on whom the United States forced a ban on poppies from 1971 to 1974, even though Turkey had virtually no opium abusers. Most ludicrous of all is the law that governs poppy growing in the United States. According to a federal statute enacted in 1971, you can't possess opium poppies, their straw, or their latex. Poppy seeds are legal, if they aren't contaminated with alkaloid-laden dust from combine harvesting. But how do you get poppy seeds without poppies?

Punishment for violating this confusing law can be a fine as high as $2,500, a jail sentence as long as ten years, or both. Fortunately, the law is mostly unenforced. Gardeners and garden-seed companies are left in peace. But the problem with a mostly unenforced law is that it can be enforced selectively at any time, as a form of persecution. Why do we stand for this?

Sadly, Americans have an unhinged love-hate relationship with opium, opiates, and opioids. The people who came to be called Boston Brahmins (the elite families Perkins, Cushing, Cabot, Forbes, Delano, and so on), after swearing off the Atlantic slave trade, made their millions in a new triangle trade based on opium. They would sail to Turkey, take Turkish opium to China, and bring Chinese silk, tea, and porcelain back to Boston. They always saved some opium for the home market, to sell to nostrum makers, who might or might not list this ingredient on their labels. Women, innocently or not, doped their colicky babies with laudanum (opium in alcohol) and grew addicted to their headache remedies. Then the Civil War came, and injured soldiers were injected with morphine, first extracted by a French chemist in 1823. Thousands acquired the "army disease," morphine addiction. Chinese laborers, who preferred smoking their opium, were run out of the country in part for a habit long fostered by the Boston Brahmins.

Around the turn of the twentieth century, scientists invented heroin, from morphine, and doctors unwittingly turned more patients into addicts. So, when World War II caused a poppy-seed shortage and California farmers tried to fill the gap, the Federal Bureau of Narcotics cracked down, first attacking a "Hindu"—an immigrant farmworker—over his poppy-straw tea, and then pursuing commercial growers. The Feds insisted that the crops be ploughed up, disked in, or otherwise destroyed. The farmers fought back in the courts for their right to grow this valuable food crop, but ultimately failed in their "Poppy Rebellion."

Today, as everyone knows, the drug companies and doctors have moved on to synthetic opioids, and yet the United States still has no sensible regulations to ensure that we can have our poppy seeds without an associated illicit drug trade. In fact, the United States has no commercial acreage devoted to poppy production at all.

Grow your own poppies, then, at your own risk, and preferably out of public view. The flowers will delight your eye and enrapture the bees, and the seeds will delectably enrich your breakfasts, snacks, and desserts. But best not slit the pods or brew them into tea.

Mohnzelten

When I visited Austria several years ago, my favorite snack was Mohnzelten, "poppy-seed tents." A specialty of the Waldviertel, the "forest quarter" northwest of Vienna, they are something like fig Newtons but bigger and round and filled with poppy seeds instead of figs.

Austrians make poppy-seed filling by first grinding the poppy seeds in a small purpose-built mill, and then mixing them with sugar and either hot milk or melted butter. I soak the poppy seeds in boiling water instead, for at least 8 hours, so they can be easily puréed in a Vitamix or another powerful blender. You can prepare the filling in advance and store it in the refrigerator or freezer until you need it.

Most Mohnzelten recipes today use chemical leavening, but I use yeast here, since I figure it is probably more traditional as well as better tasting.

Poppy-seed filling

10 ounces (283 g) poppy seeds

2 cups (473 mL) boiling water

1 ¼ cups (297 mL) whole milk

¼ cup plus 3 tablespoons (88 g) sugar

¾ teaspoon ground cinnamon

Pinch of salt

⅓ cup (113 g) honey

1 tablespoon rum

1. **To make the filling,** put the poppy seeds into a small bowl, pour the boiling water over them, and cover the bowl. Let it sit for 8 to 12 hours.

2. Drain the poppy seeds, and transfer them to a blender. Blend the mass, tamping it down as needed and adding a splash or two of the milk, if necessary. Blue seeds will turn mauve as they are ground; black seeds will turn slightly grayer. When you have a smooth purée, scoop it into a small saucepan. Add the milk, sugar, cinnamon, and salt. Heat the mixture over medium-low, stirring until it is quite thick, about 10 minutes. Turn off the heat, and stir in the honey and rum. When the mixture is cool, store it in a covered container in the refrigerator or freezer.

Dough

1 pound (454 g)
    'Makah Ozette'
    (page 121),
    russet, or other
    floury potatoes

1 cup (237 mL) milk

1 tablespoon active
    dry yeast

4 ½ cups (540 g)
    all-purpose
    flour, divided,
    plus more for
    kneading

½ cup (113 g) butter,
    softened and
    cut into chunks,
    plus more for
    greasing

3 medium egg yolks

2 teaspoons salt

3. **To make the dough,** cook the potatoes in unsalted water until they are tender. You can either peel the potatoes before cooking and afterward grate or mash them, without added liquid, or you can boil them in their skins and then press them through a ricer, leaving the skins behind. The latter method works better with 'Makah Ozette' potatoes. If the riced potatoes seem too firm to quickly blend into a smooth dough, mash them with a potato masher.

4. While the potatoes cook, warm the milk to 105 to 115°F (41 to 46°C). Pour the milk into a medium bowl, and sprinkle the yeast over the surface. Wait about 5 minutes for the yeast to soften, and then stir the mixture. Gradually stir in 2 ¼ cups (270 g) of the flour to make a wet dough. Cover the bowl, and let the dough rise for about 25 minutes, until it is well expanded.

5. Spread the remaining 2 ¼ cups flour over a cutting board in a 12 in. (30 cm) circle. Top the flour with the dough. Add the potatoes, butter, egg yolks, and salt. Knead the ingredients for at least 10 minutes, until it turns into a soft, smooth dough, adding more flour as necessary.

6. Butter a large bowl, add the dough, cover the bowl, and set it in a warm place. Let the dough rise for 40 to 50 minutes, until it has doubled in bulk.

7. Heat the oven to 400°F (200°C).

8. Punch down the dough. On a lightly floured cutting board, divide the dough into sixteen pieces. Form the pieces into balls, and cover them with a cloth. One at a time, spread each ball into a circle about 5 ½ in. (14 cm) wide, using your fingers or a rolling pin. Place ¼ cup (60 mL) of poppy-seed filling in the center. Pull up on opposite sides—at top and bottom, left and right, and then diagonally, twice—to enclose the filling. Turn the ball over, and flatten it to about 3 ½ in. (9 cm) wide. Place it on an ungreased baking sheet. Form the rest of the Mohnzelten the same way, and place them about 2 in. (5 cm) apart on baking sheets. After all the Mohnzelten are formed, let them rise for about 10 minutes.

9. Bake the Mohnzelten for about 15 minutes, until they are lightly browned on top. Remove each pan from the oven, turn the Mohnzelten over, and bake them for about 10 minutes longer, until they are golden brown on both sides.

10. Transfer the Mohnzelten to a rack. Let them cool before serving them. They store well in the freezer.

Beets
for Greens

Ever-present in my backyard vegetable garden is chard, the beet grown only for its top. To the delight of the lazy gardener, chard survives and even thrives with little to no irrigation, and it grows happily in almost any sort of dirt, including alkaline and salty soils (one article suggested that you can fertilize chard with salt, but I'm not going to try that). You need plant this vegetable no more than once per year, because you can harvest over and over from the same plant. When the winter is on the warm side, with temperatures seldom below 30°F (-1°C), you can keep harvesting all winter long. When the winter is somewhat colder, chard will slow its leaf production nearly to a standstill but begin producing generously again well before the arrival of spring.

Chard is considered biennial, but it often lives longer than two years. I had one plant, never watered, that lived five years. I think it helped that I cut down the seed stalks each year, though I rarely got around to doing so before the seeds were well developed.

I seldom plant chard; instead, I let it plant itself. Chard is self-sterile and wind-pollinated, so to get baby plants I must let at least two plants, preferably close together, go to seed. I stake the seed stalks; if I didn't the plants would become sprawling masses, burying other plants around them. The seeds come in clusters of as many as five (but usually fewer), in a hard shell that looks like a rough, almost spiny ball. Eventually these balls fall to the ground, and in the spring new plants come up.

If I want to start plants myself, or share the seeds, I strip the dry, brown clusters from the stalks and store them like other seeds. Soaking the clusters for several hours or overnight aids germination. The seedlings transplant easily, so I usually start them in flats in the greenhouse. If extra plants grow from a cluster, I snip or pinch them off.

If you're saving beet seeds, don't let your chard flower, or your beet seedlings may all grow up as chard, not beet. That's because chard and beet are two variants of the same species. They started out as *Beta vulgaris* subsp. *maritima*, the sea beet or wild beet, a low-growing plant that may have originated in Sicily but that, thousands of years ago, was already growing all around the shores of the Mediterranean. The plant eventually made its way up the Atlantic coast of Europe all the way to the British Isles, and eastward across Asia Minor and the Caucasus. Red variants occurred even in Aristotle's time. Theophrastus and Dioscorides described two forms, "white" and "black," with light and dark green leaves, respectively. (The first would ease the bowels, wrote Dioscorides; the second would bind them. Both were supposed to be good for earaches, dandruff, and lice, and the boiled root for pustules and burns.)

Beets with swollen, fleshy roots developed later. Even today Italians call beets grown for their roots *barbabietola*, "beet beard," which implies that the roots are stringy, as indeed beetroots once were. Ancient Romans sometimes used the roots, but only as medicine. Later, by the sixteenth century, beets with round, red roots had been developed. Between 1515 and 1518, such beets, along with other vegetables, fruits, and flowers, were pictured in murals in the Roman mansion now known as Villa Farnesina. Whether round beetroots originated in Italy or farther north is unknown, but in any case the French, Germans, and English came to call them Roman beets.

Bigger beetroots developed in Central Europe, home of the *mangold-wurzel*, a name usually shortened to *mangold* or, more often, *mangel* (*mangold* is the original German name for chard; *wurzel* means root). Reddish-yellow in color, mangel roots sometimes grow to forty pounds or more. From the mangel, in the eighteenth century, Prussian scientists developed the sugar beet, and then quickly bred it to such a high sugar content that it became an economical alternative to sugarcane. The fodder beet, like the mangel but sweeter, probably originated from a cross between a mangel and a sugar beet.

It's unclear when chard with broad leaf stems, or petioles, originated, but this happened before Johanne Bauhino (or Jean Bauhin), a Swiss botanist,

wrote his *Historia Plantarum Universalis*. Bauhin died in 1613, leaving the book unfinished, but it was eventually completed by another botanist and published in 1651. In the book Bauhin described two sorts of *betae*, one of them *beta laticaulis monstrosa*, "monstrous wide-stemmed beet."

More than a century later, the English plantsman Thomas Mawe, apparently wishing to honor his Swiss predecessor, described the "great white Swiss Beet, having very broad leaves, with thick foot stalks and ribs." The petioles, he wrote, were "great improvers of soup, also for stewing, and to be dressed and eaten like asparagus."

The French especially took to those petioles, which reminded them of *cardon*—that is, cardoon, the artichoke bred for its leaf stems. So the French called Swiss chard *bette*, or *blette, à carde*.

But chard was even better than cardoon in some respects. Cardoon stems are tied together and blanched for about three weeks before they are eaten. Swiss chard stems could be harvested over a much longer period, and no blanching was necessary.

This is not to say that the French disdained the green part of the chard leaf. The people of Nice have long eaten such quantities of chard, leaf stems and greens both, that they traditionally call themselves, in the local dialect, *caga blea*, "chard pooper." They even make a dessert pie of chard greens, with apples and rum-soaked raisins.

By 1843, English writers had rendered the French *carde* as *chard*. But U.S. seed sellers at first recognized only one chard variety, which they alternatively named Swiss chard, spinach beet, and silver beet (typical catalog entries were "Swiss Chard, or Spinach Beet" and "Silver or Spinach Beet"). In the twentieth century they began selling chard cultivars: 'Lucullus', from Italy, and Burpee's 'Fordhook Giant' and 'Rhubarb', with its red leaf stems and veins. Late in the century, yellow- and pink-stemmed cultivars were introduced as well. But missing from most seed catalogs was chard closer to its ancestral roots, without the big petioles.

In my kitchen, I use great quantities of chard greens, but I dislike the petioles. They are tasty enough raw; they're crisp like celery but juicier, and pleasantly sweet. Even more so than celery, though, they're stringy, especially if they're big. To avoid chewing on a wad of string, you must string each stem before you eat it, by loosening the outer fibers at one cut end and gently stripping them down the length.

Besides eating them raw, however, I have never quite known what to do with chard stems. Spaniards boil the stems, roll them in flour and egg, and fry them, but the results, to my mind, fail to justify the mess. Italians boil the stems nearly to mush—for thirty minutes, according to the esteemed cookbook author Marcella Hazan—and then sauté them with garlic or bake them with butter and cheese. The French traditionally cook them in butter, cream, or béchamel, all of which strike me as too white and too fatty. In parts of France, say the authors of *Preserving Food without Freezing or Canning*, chard stems are traditionally fermented in a weak brine without seasonings. After trying the recipe, though, I made a one-word marginal note: "Yuck."

One year I tried pickling white-chard stems in vinegar, with pretty good results, though I learned that stringing the stems is even more important when you're pickling them than when you're eating them raw, because the strings tend to separate from the flesh during pickling and become immediately irritating in the mouth. The next year I made the same pickle but with the 'Bright Lights' cultivar, with its assortment of beautiful yellows, pinks, and reds. Unfortunately, 'Bright Lights' turned out to be just as stringy as plain white-stemmed chard. And the color on the yellow, pink, and red stems, I found out, was only skin deep, and much of it came off with stringing. My 'Bright Lights' had dimmed before the pickling began. The next day I had another surprise: All the contents of the jar were a very pale pink. The chard had given up its color to its pickling liquid. I might as well have pickled a jar full of white-stemmed chard and slipped in a small slice of beet.

Pickled chard stems aren't bad, but there is plenty else in the world to pickle, and if I never ate another chard stem in my life I wouldn't regret it. So, I was thrilled when someone gave me a seed packet, from Italy, of a kind of chard called *liscia verde da taglio* ("smooth green cutting"). Pictured on the packet were chard plants with relatively flat, tender leaves and thin stems. While my daughter was living in France, she had told me about this chard, which she much preferred to the broad-stemmed types, and I'd seen it myself in an Italian market. To use the leaves of regular chard—for which I now reserve the qualifier *Swiss*—you must carve the green part of the leaf away from the tough, stringy petiole. With verde da taglio, you simply cut off the stems with one whack. The smooth leaves of verde da taglio are easier to clean, too; you don't have to uncrumple them and turn up their edges, as you must savoyed Swiss chard leaves, to check for insect cocoons. And the leaves of verde da taglio seem to have a somewhat milder taste, too. They are a better substitute for spinach than Swiss chard leaves.

For the past several years, verde da taglio is the only variety of chard I've grown in my garden. I've been delighted when it has produced red offspring, though it may have done so by crossing with a red beetroot plant. No matter. Except in color, verde da taglio and beet greens are little different. They can be used interchangeably.

Chard leaves can be cooked and used in any way you might use cooked spinach. I admit they are usually more bitter, but you can overcome that bitterness with sweetness—from well-cooked bulb onions, say, or with raisins and pine nuts, as in the classic Catalan preparation. Acid works, too; the juice as well as zest of a lemon enhances chard delightfully. The taste will be much milder still if you eat the plant very young, as a microgreen.

Even if you devour chard until you turn green, you may well grow more than you can eat fresh. In this case you might freeze some leaves to eat during the few months that your plants may not produce. The first time I considered freezing chard I hesitated, because the thought of frozen chard reminds me of frozen spinach, which my mother used to buy in a paper box, thaw in a saucepan, and plop onto plates while my father sang that he was Popeye the Sailor Man and I turned white (we children were forced to eat whatever was served). But frozen spinach is little different from cooked fresh spinach, and frozen chard is little different from frozen spinach. You can use frozen chard in puréed soups, chunky soups like minestrone, lasagna, tossed pasta, crêpes, quiche, saag paneer, spanakopita, and much else. And how handy, on busy days, to have cooked chard in a form that needs only thawing. No disposing of snails and slugs, no washing, no cutting out petioles. Just thaw the stuff, and it's ready to incorporate into dinner.

Freezing chard is simple: Wash the leaves well; cut off the stems (cut the stems *out of* large Swiss chard leaves); and cut the bigger leaves into pieces. You don't need to chop the leaves; you would lose more nutrients that way, and big pieces allow you more flexibility when you take the chard out of the freezer. In a kettle of boiling water, blanch the leaves in batches for two minutes. Drain the chard; chill it in cold water; drain it again; and pack it into freezer-weight plastic bags or rigid containers. Use the now-greenish blanching water for soup or give it to thirsty plants in your garden.

Chard *with* Raisins *and* Pine Nuts

SERVES 3

For a heartier dish, add *jamón serrano*, other dry-cured ham, or cooked bacon, diced, and sauté briefly before adding the pine nuts. If you're using cooked chard from the freezer, thaw it, and skip the boiling step. Coarsely chop the chard before adding it to the pan.

3 tablespoons raisins

1 pound (454 g) chard leaves, petioles
  removed, large leaves halved or quartered

Salt

3 tablespoons olive oil

¼ cup (40 g) minced onion

2 garlic cloves, minced

3 tablespoons pine nuts

1. Put the raisins into a small bowl, and cover them with boiling water. Bring a pot of salted water to a boil. Add the chard leaves to the water, and boil them until tender, about 5 minutes.

2. Drain the chard, pressing lightly with a spoon to remove excess water. Coarsely chop the leaf mass, and set it aside.

3. Heat the olive oil in a skillet over medium heat. Add the onion, and sauté until it is soft, about 10 minutes. Add the garlic, and sauté briefly, until it is fragrant. Stir in the pine nuts, and sauté briefly.

4. Drain the raisins, and add them to the skillet along with the chard. Continue cooking and stirring until all the ingredients are heated through. Add salt to taste. Serve immediately in a heated dish.

Forgotten *but* Flavorful Quince

When we bought our little bungalow, on a city lot in Lebanon, Oregon, the first tree I planted was a quince. The lot is small, it had no fruit trees at all, and I wanted to plant as many types as would fit in the sunny front yard. But I valued the quince over all others.

The quince had become part of my identity. Ever since planting two 'Pineapple' quince trees on our farm, I had experimented with the uncommon fruit. I made quince jelly, preserves, jam (in red and white), syrup, sauce, chutney, liqueur, wine, desserts, and, especially, paste—that is, thick, sliceable jam, the original marmalade, best known today by the Spanish name for quince, *membrillo*. I combined quince with other fruits in jellies, pastes, and so on. I wandered the quince rows at the USDA Germplasm Repository in Corvallis at harvest time, happily biting into fruits that are supposedly inedible raw and comparing the tastes of the many different cultivars. I wrote extensively about my quince experiments. I wanted everyone to know how good quinces were.

My quince trees first seduced me with their beauty. Quince trees grow no more than 15 ft. (4.6 m) high, and each forms an umbrella-like canopy. The trees blossom profusely, with pale pink flowers that are bigger than apple and pear blossoms. My trees' springtime appearance was outdone only by

their glory in autumn, when their hundreds of big, golden, pear-shaped fruits perfumed the garden with a pineapple-like scent (the aroma of quinces is so attractive and powerful that some people keep a quince in the house or car just to perfume the air). The harvest is late, not until November, just in time for Thanksgiving. Picking quinces epitomizes the joy and sadness of the season, because quinces in the house are no longer on the tree.

By the 1940s, quince trees had mostly vanished from American gardens. Before the invention of packaged pectin, though, nearly every American farmstead, where the climate allowed, had a tree like mine, because quince is an excellent source of pectin. The tart, light-colored juice combines well with other fruits and juices and with spices such as ginger, cinnamon, nutmeg, and cardamom. The fruit is hard and mildly astringent, but when cooked it mellows and softens, without losing its shape, and with long cooking it turns from white to a startling ruby red. Only the cook's creativity can limit the variety of beautiful jams, jellies, and preserves she can produce with quinces.

But quinces are useful for much more than gelled preserves. You can poach the fruits in wine and honey, roast them with vegetables, stew them with meats, bake them like apples, and cook them in pies, crisps, and sauce, with or without other fruits. Clear, golden quince syrups and liqueurs are as distinct and delicious as their raspberry and black-currant counterparts. And you can make all these delectable foods with the harvest of one mature tree.

And one tree is probably all you'll need, if you want to grow quinces, because your tree will not only yield abundantly; it will also self-pollinate. (I planted two quince trees on the farm by mistake, though I never regretted the error.)

What variety of quince should you choose? Cultivars differ in the size and shape of the fruit—some fruits are round rather than pear-shaped—and some, such as 'Portugal', tend to redden more readily with cooking. But I found little difference in flavor or texture among the many cultivars at the Germplasm Repository. I love my 'Pineapple', but I don't find the fruits as distinct as the breeder, Luther Burbank, made them out to be, in either aroma or tenderness. To me, *all* quinces smell like pineapple. And if "the Pineapple quince when thoroughly ripe rivals the apple as a fruit to be eaten raw," as Burbank insisted, I must wonder if my fruits have ever been thoroughly ripe. I do eat them raw, in small pieces, but I don't gobble them down like apples. Perhaps there are varieties more tender and without any astringency at all; for example, Jim Gilbert claimed that at least two of the quinces he brought from Russia in the

1990s ('Aromatnaya' and 'Kuganskaya') could be eaten straight from the tree. But I think that the quince-that-needs-no-cooking may be partially mythical, and I wonder why we need such a myth. I found all the quinces at the Germplasm Repository decent for a raw bite or two, and great for cooking. So, if you have little choice among quinces varieties, don't worry—just get a quince tree. 'Pineapple', 'Orange', 'Smyrna', and 'Van Deman' (another Burbank cultivar) are all easy to find in the United States, and they are well tested and beloved. And some of Jim Gilbert's Russian varieties are still available from the nursery he founded, One Green World.

Your quince tree won't demand much care. Once established, it will tolerate drought well. You won't have to spray your tree, because the hard fruit resists both apple maggots and coddling moths. Leaf blight can occur, but only where summers are wet. You'll want to do some annual pruning, because quinces often branch chaotically, sideways and backward. But otherwise, your quince tree will take care of itself.

Now that my front-yard quince tree has reached full production, my husband and I are using most of the fruit in savory dishes. If you don't have much of a sweet tooth or you're tired of making preserves, I suggest roasting some quinces with vegetables. Serve the mixture with roast meat and a salad, and you have a complete and easy celebratory dinner.

Roasted Quinces *and* Sweet Potatoes

SERVES ABOUT 4

Unripe quinces are usually covered with a woolly substance, much of which comes off on its own as the fruits ripen. Rub off the remainder before cutting your quinces.

Because the quince is a very hard fruit, you'll want to cut it with a heavy blade. Halve it lengthwise and set the two halves face down before slicing them into quarters (or eighths, if the quinces are very large). Core each piece. For coring you can use a sturdy paring knife or, to avoid the risk of cutting through the wedge, you might prefer a pitting spoon, a pointed spoon with sharpened sides.

Despite their high acid content, quinces quickly brown when cut. You can protect the slices for a time by holding them in water acidulated with lemon juice or ascorbic acid, but I just put them promptly into the oven.

I don't bother to peel either the sweet potatoes or quinces, but you can peel them if you like. You might substitute winter squash, carrots, or parsnips for the sweet potatoes in this recipe, or use a mix of these vegetables.

1 pound (454 g) sweet potatoes, cut into wedges
    or chunks

1 pound (454 g) quinces, cut into wedges or chunks
    to match the sweet potatoes, and cored

2 tablespoons olive oil

Salt

Small rosemary branch (optional)

1. Heat the oven to 425°F (220°C). Spread the sweet potatoes and quinces in a roasting pan. Pour the olive oil over, and toss together until everything is coated. Sprinkle with salt to taste. Add the rosemary, if desired, for an even more aromatic dish.

2. Roast the mixture for 20 to 30 minutes, until the sweet potatoes and quinces are tender. If the pieces start to char before this point, turn them gently.

3. Serve the mixture hot, perhaps with roast turkey or lamb.

Oca, *the* Tart Little Tuber

I first planted oca, a South American wood sorrel, after my friend Rose Marie Nichols McGee gave me two little pink tubers one spring. Because the plant is sensitive to day length, Rose Marie explained, the tubers are produced in mid-October in our region—*if* the plant is protected from frost. This posed a problem for me, since in past years the first frost had hit my garden in early October. I decided to plant the ocas in a big pot on the deck, where I'd be sure to keep an eye on them.

The plants grew no more than 18 in. (46 cm) tall before flopping onto their sides. The stems were fleshy and the leaves clover-like, resembling other foliage in the *Oxalis* genus. I never saw any oca flowers; I later learned they can be rare, especially where the weather is warm and dry through most of the growing season.

Before moving the pot to the greenhouse around October 1, I poked my fingers around the roots. I felt no swellings at all.

In late winter I noticed the motley assortment of pots in the middle of my greenhouse floor, all dragged there for minimal protection from the cold and now adorned with the limp, frozen foliage of various tender plants. Wasn't that droopy mess at the side of one pot the ocas? I should have checked sooner to see if the plants had produced any tubers. Kneeling on the ground, I started digging.

I pulled out a pile of tubers, some less than 1 in. (2.5 cm) long and the longest 4 in. (10 cm), each looking like a cross between a pink-skinned potato and a fat grub. Washed and dried, they looked shiny, as if rubbed with oil.

What was this strange vegetable? *Oca* is a Spanish spelling of *oqa*, which, along with *apilla*, *cuiba*, and *ibia*, is an indigenous South American name for one of several tubers traditionally farmed in the Andes. There, oca follows the potato in the customary crop rotation and assumes dietary importance at very high elevations, where potatoes don't grow well. Botanists call this tuber *Oxalis tuberosa*; Mexicans call it *papa extranjera*; and New Zealanders, who grow and consume substantial quantities, call it *yam*. (It helps to know these other names when you're searching for information about the oca, because in Spanish *oca* also means "goose.")

Like the potato, the oca comes in a range of colors—pink, red, yellow, white, and even black. Paler ocas often have darker, pink or red eyes.

Unlike the potato, the oca is generally palatable when raw. Different varieties, however, vary in their levels of oxalic acid, which can interfere with mineral absorption in the body and lead to kidney stones. In South America ocas are often treated to reduce the oxalic acid level—by setting the tubers in the sun for several days, by boiling them, or, in the case of high-oxalate varieties, by first fermenting and then freeze-drying them.

This doesn't mean ocas aren't good for you. They are rich in carbohydrates and iron, they have a higher vitamin C content than potatoes, and some varieties have ample carotene. Ocas also contain a soluble protein called ocatin, which has antifungal and antibacterial properties. And the oxalic acid in the tubers isn't normally a concern in North America, since in the varieties available here the oxalate content of the tubers is low, comparable to that of garlic, carrots, Brussels sprouts, and snap beans.

I had to taste some of my ocas right away. They were crisp as an apple straight from the tree, not sweet, but pleasant. Some had a slight sorrel taste; others were quite tart. Inside, the flesh was light golden. I left the remaining ocas in a bowl in front of a window for several days, turning them occasionally, but (as often happens during western Oregon winters) the sun never came out.

I figured I'd better cook the rest before I absentmindedly ate them all raw.

So, how to cook my ocas? Ecuadorians, I learned, preserve ocas in syrup and combine them with berries in jam. Columbians serve boiled *ibias*, as they call them, with tomato-and-onion salsa. They also cook them with eggs in something like a Spanish tortilla, make them into jam, puddings, and cakes, and, most often, use them for *chicha*, a beverage of grain or root vegetables fermented with cane syrup and water.

I'd harvested a mere 9 ounces (255 g) of ocas, and I wanted to save some for planting, so I had only about 4 ounces (113 g) to spare. The recipes I found sounded either impractical for such a small quantity or, with the cupboard still full of Christmas sweets, too sugary to have much appeal. So I decided to use my ocas as I do so many other small pickings from the garden: in a stir-fry. I combined the oca with tofu and ham and served the mixture over steamed mizuna. The oca skins lost most of their color with cooking, and afterward I felt that I'd cooked the tubers too long, so they lost their crispness. But still I deemed the dish a success. The stir-fried oca tasted a lot like water chestnut, though less sweet.

Since then, we've had oca every year. I usually put some of the smaller tubers in a paper bag in the basement to plant out in spring. Even if I don't store any tubers over the winter, a few I've missed digging will produce a crop the following year. (Leaving ocas in the ground won't work if your ground freezes more than about ⅜ in., or 1 cm, deep.)

I haven't planted ocas in a pot again, though the plants would be attractive enough in combination with a taller ornamental. Instead, I grow them in the ground, in any little space where I can fit them. I try to make sure the plants get a little water, because they do like plenty of moisture, although they also need good drainage.

My oca crop is always small, partially because I give my plants little attention (I probably don't water them enough, and I don't protect them from frosts) and partially because oca just isn't especially productive. Bill Whitson, a plant breeder, says that ocas can produce three pounds of tubers per plant in a favorable climate but that the usual yield, outside of the Andes, is about a pound. He also says that oca tubers can grow up to 8 in. (20 cm) long. Mine never exceed 4 in. (10 cm).

Besides keeping the soil moist, I could probably improve my yield in other ways. For the largest oca crop, Whitson advises, a gardener should delay harvest—and protect the plants from frost—until the second week in November. This is because ocas don't start forming tubers until there is less than twelve hours of daylight. And William Woys Weaver has a trick I haven't tried: He says he triples his crop by burying the stems in soil, as with potatoes.

Because I'm growing oca as an occasional winter treat, not as a dietary staple, I'm happy with the small crop I get. In case you grow a lot of ocas, both Whitson and Weaver have other suggestions for using them. Weaver says they're good grilled, fried, and dried. Whitson likes to drizzle the tubers with oil and roast them at 350°F (175°C). He also eats the stems and leaves. They are more acidic than the tubers and so probably shouldn't be consumed in large quantity, but the raw leaves can be added to salads, and he uses the stems as a substitute for rhubarb or gooseberries in pie.

One of my favorite uses for oca is as a vegetable in stew. In curries and other stews, oca tubers please me more than potatoes, which I find too mealy no matter what kind of potato I choose. I use small, whole oca tubers, and they always remain intact, although with long cooking their insides become very soft. I like the contrast of the firm, smooth skin with the soft interior.

Rockfish Curry *with* Oca *and* Winter Squash

SERVES 3

Rockfish is not a particular species but a general category of fish that are common along the Oregon coast. Some are long-lived and rare, others short-lived, plentiful, and inexpensive. We find only the latter in local stores. The flavor of these fish is mild, but I really like their slightly chewy texture. You can substitute other white fish, chicken, turkey, or firm tofu in this recipe.

When I use leeks rather than onions, I include the green part as well as the white, but I discard any thick, fibrous leaf tops. Chopped and blanched leeks store well in the freezer.

1 tablespoon peanut or other vegetable oil

1 large onion or leek (about 8 oz. or 227 g), chopped

3 to 4 tablespoons Mae Ploy Thai curry paste (yellow, green, or a combination)

1 cup (237 mL) water

10 ounces (283 g) peeled dense winter squash, such as red kuri, cut into 1 in. (2.5 cm) pieces

6 ounces (170 g) small oca tubers

1 stalk lemongrass, cut diagonally into large pieces (optional)

One 13.5 ounce (400 mL) can coconut milk (for a lighter curry) or coconut cream (for a richer curry)

Fish sauce, shrimp paste, or salt

1 turmeric root, finely grated (optional)

12 ounces (340 g) rockfish, cut into 1 in. (2.5 cm) pieces

Cooked jasmine rice, for serving

2 tablespoons chopped cilantro leaves, for serving (optional)

1. Heat the oil in a large pot set over medium heat. Add the onion, and sauté until tender. Add the curry paste, and use a wooden spoon or spatula to blend the paste with the onion. Add the water, and bring it to a simmer, stirring to break up any remaining clumps of curry paste. Add the squash, oca, and lemongrass. The vegetables should be barely covered by the water; add more water if needed. Cover the pot, and simmer the vegetables until the squash is just tender.

2. With the pot still over the heat, stir in the coconut milk. Taste for salt (the curry paste has quite a lot), and add fish sauce as needed. Add the grated turmeric, if using. When the sauce is heated through, add the fish. Turn it gently and occasionally until it is cooked through; this should take no more than a few minutes.

3. Serve the curry over jasmine rice, garnished, if you like, with chopped cilantro.

243

Jerusalem Fartichokes

Does your spouse refuse to eat Jerusalem artichokes because they're too—err—windy? Have you yourself abandoned your Jerusalem artichoke patch to the weeds or the pigs, because no human of your acquaintance would eat the damn things again? If so, you have plenty of company.

If you can't quite place this native North American vegetable, you may know it instead by the name invented by a California produce wholesaler in the 1960s: the sunchoke. The *sun* part of this moniker comes from *sunflower*, because the plant belongs to the same genus as the sunflower that provides us seeds for birds, snacks, and oil. Jerusalem artichoke blooms look like small sunflowers, and the plants can grow just as tall as the tallest annual sunflower stalks. But the Jerusalem artichoke tends to multiply not by dropping its seeds and offering them to birds, but by spreading its underground rhizomes and forming tubers.

The *Jerusalem* part of *Jerusalem artichoke* came about soon after the plants were brought to France from Canada, in the early seventeenth century. By 1613 Petrus Hondius was growing and breeding the tubers in Terneuzen, Netherlands, and several years later they arrived in England. There the "artichoke-apples of Terneuzen" acquired the name Jerusalem, either because it sounded more appealing and exotic than *Terneuzen* or because someone translated *sunflower* to the Latin *girasole* and someone else misinterpreted that word as *Jerusalem*. In either case, the name stuck. Louis Eustache Ude invented "potage à la

Palestine" in 1841, and soon cooks all over England were making their Jerusalem artichokes into "Palestine soup."

Sunroot would be a better name for the vegetable than sunchoke, because Jerusalem artichokes certainly are not artichokes, and they have nothing like the hairy, inedible part of an artichoke that is called the choke. Yet the two vegetables known as artichoke are discreetly similar in their chemical makeup and flavor. Samuel de Champlain noted this in 1605, when he found Abenaki Indians on Cape Cod growing roots with "le goust d'artichaut," the taste of artichokes. Both artichokes and Jerusalem artichokes, he may have observed, share a peculiar sweetness. This sweetness comes from inulin, a kind of soluble fiber that passes through the human digestive system intact until bacteria break it down in the colon, releasing a lot of gas in the process. Artichokes are rich in inulin. Jerusalem artichokes have about 50 percent more, by percentage of fresh weight.

Gardeners love to plant Jerusalem artichokes, because they grow without care and produce prodigiously. The plants prefer moist alluvial soils but will withstand sand, clay, drought, and even occasional winter flooding. A single tuber, planted in spring, can yield as many as two hundred tubers in the fall.

This productivity can be problematic. How to eat Jerusalem artichokes without bringing on a bellyache has been one of the most popular subjects of discussion on my website, with the conversation continuing for more than a decade.

The dialogue started when my friend Rose Marie Nichols McGee posed a question that I should have asked myself long before: Can fermentation rid Jerusalem artichokes of their windiness? The two of us promptly decided to conduct an experiment. After digging up the little patch of Jerusalem arti-chokes that I'd ignored for ten years, I brined a pint of the tubers according to the kakdooki (Korean fermented daikon) recipe in The Joy of Pickling, with garlic and powdered chile. Rose Marie developed another recipe based on one of mine, she said, although nothing about it sounded familiar. With a stroke of brilliance, she added turmeric, so that her pickled Jerusalem artichokes turned out a brilliant yellow. We shared both pickles, hers and mine, at a Slow Food board meeting, and people seemed to find them both tasty. I requested follow-up digestive reports.

But I got none. Was this good news? I couldn't be sure. Nobody's bellyache was bad enough to prompt a complaint. But the meeting attendees hadn't actually agreed to tell me about their gas problems. Some of them may have felt they didn't know me well enough. And none of them had eaten more than a small handful of the pickled tubers. Our study was inconclusive.

In digging up my Jerusalem artichoke patch, I must have missed a little tuber. The next summer, sans weeding and sans water, a single 9 ft. (2.7 m) stalk shot up. I could experiment some more!

I waited through most of the winter to dig up the tubers, because time alone has been said to convert much of the inulin in Jerusalem artichokes to fructose (though fructose, too, is hard for many people to digest). In January I harvested a crop just as big as the previous year's, at least ten pounds. Several nights of temperatures around 0°F (-18°C) had done the tubers no harm. I loaded them into a galvanized washtub and hosed them clean.

Now, how best to cook them, I wondered, while avoiding "a filthy loathsome stinking winde" (as John Goodyer described the tubers' aftereffects in 1621)? I consulted Harold McGee. In *The Curious Cook*, McGee advises steaming Jerusalem artichokes in an oven at 200°F (93°C) for twenty-four hours to break down the inulin into fructose. This was a way of mimicking pit cooking, the method Western tribes used for camas, another gassy root vegetable. But McGee's method, to me, seemed an extravagant use of fuel, and anyhow his artichokes turned out black (the blackening had to do with Jerusalem artichokes' high iron content).

I tried long, slow cooking in a slow cooker instead, but the tubers turned out so unpleasant in taste and appearance that I understood why the English doctor Tobias Venner, in 1620, wrote that Jerusalem artichokes "breedeth melancholy."

Next, I tried roasting some of the tubers, with salt, black pepper, and olive oil, in the way you would usually roast vegetables, but slower, at 350°F (175°C) for two hours. Perhaps this would be long enough, I thought, to make the tubers more digestible. And what a delicious dish they turned out to be! The chunks were crunchy on the outside and soft and candy-sweet on the inside. Robert thought they would make an excellent side for roast beef.

But still the rumbles followed.

I then fermented some tubers in a pickle something like Rose Marie's, with ginger and cumin as well as turmeric. These three spices are all said to be carminative—that is, relieving of gas and bloating. Several people ate this pickle in potentially distressing quantities. The test subjects remained on site this time, so that if reports didn't come verbally they would emerge in another audible form. And nobody suffered.

I published the recipe on my website and got more positive reports, along with many recommendations and much speculation. Try cooking the tubers with *bonenkruid*—summer savory—wrote someone from the Netherlands. Try asafoetida, wrote a parent of three bean-eating boys. Boil the tubers with a potato, suggested a European of some kind. Genetics will determine your degree of suffering, somebody submitted. Introduce Jerusalem artichokes into your diet slowly, advised another. A student planned to prepare the tubers in various ways "and make graphs (farts per unit of time)."

At least one reader was indignant: Inulin is good for you! After all, it is extracted and sold as a nutritional supplement for the diabetic, the obese, and the constipated. Inulin helps control insulin. Inulin may help prevent cancer of the colon, the rectum, and even the breast.

But one reader found that not all inulin is alike. She had used chicory inulin as a digestive supplement with no problem, but Jerusalem artichoke inulin was another matter: "The pain in my stomach!!!" In fact, Wikipedia informed me, inulin is "a heterogeneous collection of fructose polymers," with long, short, and, sometimes, branched fructose chains. Since plant species vary in their inulin composition, it makes sense that inulin from different plant sources could affect people differently.

Surely it helps your gut microbiome to adjust your diet gradually, but some individuals seem inherently better able to tolerate inulin than others. Even John Goodyer noted that although Jerusalem artichokes "are a meat more fit for swine than men: yet some say they have usually eaten them, and have found no such windy qualitie in them." My daughter, who lives in Sweden, says that Swedes eat a lot of Jerusalem artichokes, and nobody she asks says they cause any gas (believe me: she does not hesitate to ask). The difference could be genetic, or perhaps Swedes are more accustomed to more inulin in their diets year-round, maybe because they eat bread and crackers made primarily of rye, which is richer in inulin than wheat.

It could be that Swedes grow, or eat, Jerusalem artichokes that are unusually low in inulin. A low inulin content could be due to growing conditions, breeding, or both. The plants come in many varieties, which differ in inulin content as well as in the height of the plant; the size, shape, and color of the tubers (many are red or purple instead of white); and in the thickness of the tubers'

skins. Europeans, especially French and Russian breeders, have developed numerous cultivars. In North America, where Jerusalem artichokes originated, we also have many varieties, though you would be hard-pressed to find more than the basic white one in seed and plant catalogs. Members of Seed Savers Exchange, however, list plenty of others. Unfortunately, nobody seems to describe the varieties for sale by inulin content.

I didn't plan to grow Jerusalem artichokes after we moved into the city, but someone offered me a big, beautiful white tuber, and I couldn't resist. Attempting to keep the harvest small, I planted the tuber in a shady corner where the plant would receive no supplemental water, and I tried to confine it with landscape fabric. The next winter my production was higher than it had ever been on the farm. My experiments continued, and so did the discussion on my website.

I remembered the first "artichoke pickle" I'd ever eaten, a mixed vinegar pickle, like chowchow, that somebody's Southern grandma had made. It took me a long time to understand that the pickle contained nothing that I would call simply *artichoke*, but eventually I identified the little chunks of tuber. Since then, I'd studied various recipes similar to the grandma's, so I knew they always included a soaking or boiling step. Harold McGee confirmed that inulin is highly soluble in water. It must be the inulin that makes the bubbles appear strangely large when you boil Jerusalem artichokes; the stuff apparently acts as a surfactant. McGee boiled his Jerusalem artichokes for fifteen minutes and figured he had drawn out 40 to 50 percent of the "indigestibles"—the powdery residue left in the pan after he had boiled off the water.

Unfortunately, I don't like the taste of boiled Jerusalem artichokes. I find the tubers much tastier raw, roasted, or fried. Judiciously combined with other vegetables, though, boiled Jerusalem artichokes can add appeal. So I boiled some of the tubers to mix with mashed potatoes. I routinely boil potatoes as my mother and grandmother did, with only a little water, so the pan ends up dry when the potatoes are ready, and no nutrients are lost in the water. To reduce the inulin in the Jerusalem artichokes, though, I gave them a different treatment: I put them into a separate pan, covered them with water, boiled them for about fifteen minutes, and then threw out all the water. The artichokes don't soften as potatoes do, but if you peel them before or after boiling them (peeling them first is more trouble but may help them shed more inulin) you can force them through a ricer. Without drawing too much attention to themselves, the Jerusalem artichokes nicely sweetened the starchy, dry pota-toes. (The Jerusalem artichokes announced their presence more aggressively, but tolerably, some hours later.)

I boiled more Jerusalem artichokes in the same way, and then riced and froze them. I would use them in potages with spinach, leeks, celery, or sorrel—delicious variations on Palestine soup.

Next, I decided to try making chips. For the first trial batch, I sliced the tubers thin and soaked them for thirty minutes in water with salt and lemon juice stirred in. This soaking, I hoped, would both prevent browning and give the chips extra savor. Then I dried the slices in the dehydrator until they turned leathery. These chips turned out pale and uninteresting. So I baked them in the oven at 200°F (93°C) until they were golden brown. Now, to my delight, they were sweet and crisp.

But I couldn't taste the salt. Also, I concluded that the lemon juice had been unnecessary, since raw Jerusalem artichokes seem disinclined to brown with exposure to air. For the next batch I soaked the slices for an hour in a brine made of ¼ cup (65 g) pickling salt to 2 cups (473 mL) water. I skipped the dehydration step; instead, I put the slices straight into the convection oven.

The second batch turned out as good as the first, with a bit of saltiness added. I imagined that they would have been just as good with no salt at all. Besides, keeping the chips salt-free might discourage overconsumption—and overconsumption would be risky if the drying and baking failed to overcome the vegetable's gassiness.

I tested the chips on people at an afternoon political meeting. Everybody seemed to like them, and none could guess what they were made of. Two people were gracious enough to take home small bagfuls, eat all the chips in a sitting, and report the results. One of them told me that "right around 10 p.m. it hit. They weren't particularly odorous or loud, just little bubbly poots all night, and that was pretty much the end of it." The other reported, "If I knowingly eat this food again, I will plan on working around loud machinery, or going on a hike by myself. Bottom line, they taste good."

The next year I tried frying the chips. The fried chips, I figured, would be even tastier than the baked ones. They would be less trouble to make, and they would allow me to use a large quantity of tubers quickly.

In the end I was glad I'd cooked a lot of tubers, because the chips shrank substantially; they lost two-thirds of their weight. They turned out curled and

brown, a sweet, salty, crisp, greasy delight. They still had pooty powers, but Robert and I didn't suffer much if we restricted ourselves to a handful a day. (This takes discipline. The chips are addictive!)

A reader informed me of his wife's success in taming Jerusalem artichokes this way: She sliced them, soaked the slices in lightly salted water overnight, rinsed them, put them into a pot of fresh water, and brought it just to a boil. Then she drained the slices and stir-fried them. They turned out crisp and tasty but not gassy.

This made me think again of the Southern "artichoke pickle." Perhaps soaking or boiling should be a standard pretreatment before frying, baking, or vinegar-pickling Jerusalem artichokes. Several scientific studies on inulin extraction from Jerusalem artichokes recommend fifteen- to sixty-five-minute soaks at 122 to 176°F (60 to 80°C).

These scientists, however, aren't interested in the digestibility of Jerusalem artichokes; they only want to know how best to extract the inulin. They grind the tubers and dry them before soaking them. With this method they claim a yield of inulin as high as 92.5 percent. With bigger pieces of tuber, you won't extract as much.

Could a long soak in cool water followed by a brief boil work? I tested my reader's wife's method on a pint of sliced tubers. I concluded that Jerusalem artichokes are a fair substitute for water chestnuts in a stir-fry. And the aftereffects, for Robert and me, were mild, so mild that they may have been caused by the accompanying Chinese cabbage and leek.

I also tried making fried chips with boiled tubers. I simmered the slices for fifteen minutes, drained them, fried them—and then ate them all at once. Through the double cooking process, they seemed to lose some sweetness and some substance, too; I didn't weigh them before and after, but they turned out diaphanous. Amazingly, I experienced no aftereffects at all. But, as I was the only test subject, further tests are needed. I'm afraid that at this point I've overwhelmed you with conflicting Jerusalem artichoke advice. So now I'll summarize how to handle your fartichokes, from harvest to stomach:

Because cold will convert some inulin to fructose, wait until winter to harvest your tubers. Dig them as you need them or harvest them all at once and store them in a cool, damp place. They will keep for weeks or months in a refrigerator, but cooler temperatures yet are required for converting inulin. I've been keeping my tubers in damp leaf mulch in an in-ground garbage can.

Fermenting your Jerusalem artichokes will indeed break down inulin; a 2021 Chinese study confirmed this. Do beware that the fermented tubers can turn out a bit slimy. To avoid this, keep the pieces quite large, and don't peel them. Fermentation may get off to a slow start, so add a little vinegar to prevent mold growth (say, 3 tablespoons vinegar in a 2 L jar). Slice the crisp, tart tubers before serving. I've had a pickle of this sort keep well in the fridge for two years.

The sweetening that occurs when you bake or fry Jerusalem artichokes proves that inulin is converting to fructose. I don't know what percentage of the inulin is converted this way, and anyhow fructose itself can be hard to digest (if apples give you gas, you are probably sensitive to fructose). In sum, expect some windiness.

A soak in hot or boiling water will extract some of the inulin from Jerusalem artichokes. A long soak in cool water may be partially effective, too. The smaller the pieces, the more inulin you'll extract. After the water treatment, the tubers may gray a bit. To prevent this, add acid (vinegar or lemon juice) to the water, or douse the tubers with acid immediately after removing them from the water. The acid treatment, of course, is appropriate only for salad or pickles.

Jerusalem artichokes soaked in hot water or even boiled for no longer than fifteen minutes can be afterward puréed, pickled in vinegar, fried, or baked, with good results. With frying or baking, the tubers will still sweeten as they brown. Expect only mild wind.

If Jerusalem artichokes don't give you a bellyache, enjoy them raw. I like to julienne them and add them to a mixed salad or serve them sliced on their own with lemon or lime juice and salt. Raw Jerusalem artichokes are delicious! Just don't eat too many.

Jerusalem Artichoke Chips, Baked *or* Fried

SERVES ABOUT 6

For the least windy chips, give your Jerusalem artichoke slices a soak in hot water before frying them. Put them in a pot of cold water and bring the water just to a boil, or bring the water first to a boil, add the slices, and keep the pot over low heat for 15 minutes. But I suggest trying baked or fried chips made as follows before concluding you need this extra step.

6 cups (1.4 L) cold water

3 tablespoons salt

3 pounds (1.4 kg) Jerusalem
   artichokes (not peeled)

Vegetable oil (optional)

1. Put the water into a bowl, and stir in the salt. Break the tubers apart at the nodes, scrub them, and slice them very thin (use a mandoline, if you have one). Drop the slices into the brine as you work. Let the slices soak in the brine for at least 1 hour and preferably 4.

2. Drain the slices well.

3. **For baked chips,** spread the slices in a single layer on wire racks set over baking pans. If you have no wire racks that the slices won't fall through, spread them directly on the baking pans. To prevent the pieces from sticking, you can oil the pan or toss the slices with a little olive oil or vegetable oil.

4. Put the pans into a convection oven heated to 200°F (93°C). If you don't have a convection oven, use a regular oven heated to 225 to 250°F (110 to 120°C). Bake the slices for 1 ¼ to 1 ½ hours, rotating the pans at least once, until the chips are almost crisp. Don't cook them so long that they turn dark brown, or they will be bitter.

5. **For fried chips,** pour at least 2 in. (5 cm) of vegetable oil into a pot, and heat the oil to 350°F (175°C). Fry the slices in batches, moving them around in the oil every now and then so they cook evenly. When the chips are shrunken, curled, and lightly browned, they are ready. This should take about 4 minutes. Drain them on paper towels, paper bags, or newspaper.

6. Spread the chips out to cool.

7. As your baked or fried chips cool, they will grow crisper. Serve them immediately, or store them in an airtight container.

NOTES

Angelica, Bitter and Sweet, pages 31 to 37

Both these angelicas: Patience Gray, *Honey from a Weed* (New York: Harper & Row, 1986), p. 203.

Strawberries from the Woods, pages 59 to 63

"Eaten with Creame and Sugar": Thomas Hill, *The Gardener's Labyrinth* (London: H. Bynneman, 1577), p. 78.

Thomas Jefferson appreciated: The letter "From Thomas Jefferson to James Monroe, 26 May 1795" is available at *Founders Online*, National Archives (founders.archives.gov/documents/Jefferson/01-28-02-0275). The other two "objects" that Jefferson referred to were the skylark and the red-legged partridge.

Kale Buds and Collard Tops, pages 77 to 81

Kids whose chewing: Damian Frank et al., "In-Mouth Volatile Production for Brassica Vegetables (Cauliflower) and Associations with Liking in an Adult/Child Cohort," *Journal of Agricultural Food Chemistry* 69, no. 39 (22 September 2021): pp. 11,646-55.

Magenta-Leafed Orach, pages 113 to 119

Given plenty of water: M. F. Babb and James E. Kraus, "Orach: Its Culture and Use as a Greens Crop in the Great Plains Region," *USDA Circular 526*, Washington, D.C. (September 1939).

Frank Morton, of Wild Garden Seeds: Carmen Porter, "*Atriplex hortensis* (Orach) with Frank Morton of Wild Garden Seed!" *Song and Plants* (Episode 23), 14 February 2022. Podcast, 20:33. song-and-plants.captivate.fm/episode/atriplex-hortensis-orach-with-frank-morton-of-wild-garden-seed.

John Gerard: *The Herball, or, Generall Historie of Plantes* (London: John Norton, 1597), pp. 256–57.

Wrapping butter: Babb and Kraus, "Orach: Its Culture and Use."

Fearing Burr, Jr.: *Field and Garden Vegetables of America* (Boston: Crosby and Nichols, 1863), p. 7.

A French researcher: U.S. Department of Agriculture Bureau of Plant Industry, "Inventory of Seeds and Plants Imported," No. 61 (Government Printing Office, Washington, D.C., 1922), pp. 9–10.

"The seeds, milled and bolted": The quote from de Noter is on p. 10 of U.S. Department of Agriculture Bureau of Plant Industry.

Birds, whose digestive systems: Porter 2022.

The Singular Makah Ozette Potato, pages 121 to 125

A 2010 DNA study: Linhai Zhang, et al., "Inferred Origin of Several Native American Potatoes from the Pacific Northwest and Southeast Alaska using SSR markers," *Euphytica* 174, no. 1 (July 2010): pp. 15–29. See also Stella Wenstob, "The Profusion of Potatoes in Pre-Colonial British Columbia," *Platforum* 12 (2011), pp. 133–60.

The Onion That Walks, pages 127 to 133

Louis le Comte: *Nouveaux Mémoires sur l'État de la Chine*, vol. 1 (Paris: Jean Annison, 1697), pp. 178–79.

John Baxter: *Library of Agricultural and Horticultural Knowledge* (London: J. Baxter, Lewes, 1830), p. 389.

Catawissa: William Woys Weaver, *Heirloom Vegetable Gardening* (New York: Henry Holt and Company, 1997), p. 232.

Black and Blue Tomatoes, pages 135 to 143

When Spanish conquerors: Kai Kupferschmidt, "How Tomatoes Lost Their Taste," *Science* (28 June 2012).

Tomatoes were often described: A. W. Livingston's "purple" tomatoes included 'Imperial', 'Acme', 'Potato Leaf', and 'Beauty'. 'Fejee Improved' was also known as 'Beefsteak', but this name was applied to other varieties as well. Around the turn of the twentieth century, the word *beefsteak* was often used to describe big, meaty tomatoes.

And then came the Russians: Gene Tempest, "Thirty Years of Russian Influence . . . on Our Tomatoes," *Boston Globe* (11 September 2019).

Bill McDorman: "The Great Siberian Adventure," *Seeds Trust* (10 June 2018). seedstrust.com/blog/2018/6/10/the-great-siberian-adventure/.

As the USSR collapsed: Kent Whealy, "Rescuing Traditional Food Crops in Eastern Europe and the Former Soviet Union," (speech at the 1993 Seed Savers Exchange Campout). cerestrust.org/rescuing-traditional-food-crops-in-eastern-europe-and-the-former-soviet-union/.

A Tennessee man: The discussion of 'Cherokee Purple' is from Craig LeHoullier's article "How the Cherokee Purple Tomato Got Its Name," accessed 1 March 2023, on slowfoodasheville.com.

USDA researchers released: Tara Weaver, "USDA Releases New Tomatoes with Increased Beta Carotene" (2 November 1998). ars.usda.gov/news-events/news/research-news/1998usda-releases-new-tomatoes-with-increased-beta-carotene/.

The Heritage Food Crops Research Trust: "The Health Potential of the 'Real' Tomato" (2013). heritagefoodcrops.org.nz/heirloom-tomatoes/the-health-potential-of-the-real-tomato/.

Even Tom Wagner: Seed Savers Exchange, "The Rise of Heirloom Seeds: Tom Wagner, Tater Mater Seeds." seedsavers.org/the-rise-of-heirloom-seeds-tom-wagner.

Jim and his team crossed red tomatoes: The thirteen or so tomato species cross easily. They used to have their own genus, *Lycopersicon*, but now botanists group them in a "section" of the same name, in the subgenus *Solanum sensu stricto* ("*Solanum* in the strict sense"). The genus *Solanum* includes the potato, the eggplant, and about 1,500 other species.

"Indigo" as part of the name: Jim Myers, "Breeding Tomatoes for Increased Flavonoids," *Organic Seed Growers Conference Proceedings* (19–21 January 2012): pp. 50–51.

The best flavor: Jim Myers, "Indigo Tomatoes: How They Came to Be and Future Prospects," Oregon State University Winter 2023 Horticulture Seminar (13 February 2023). The discussion of "Byndweed Beth" is also from this lecture.

"Tomatoes have changed": wildboarfarms.com.

The Longest Beans, pages 145 to 149

"Loose pretzly knots": Elizabeth Schneider, *Uncommon Fruits and Vegetables* (New York: Harper & Row, 1986), p. 513.

Maize for Meal, pages 165 to 169

'Glass Gem': Greg Schoen tells the story of this corn in "The Origins and Journey of 'Carl's Glass Gems' Rainbow Corn," *Mother Earth News* (13 December 2012).

Carol Deppe says: *The Resilient Gardener* (White River Junction, Vermont: Chelsea Green, 2010), p. 285.

Chicory Reborn, pages 171 to 177

A grown-up taste: Ruth Van Waerebeek's quote about learning to appreciate the bitterness of chicory is on p. 202 of *Everybody Eats Well in Belgium Cookbook* (New York: Workman, 1996).

The Many Joys of Fennel, pages 185 to 191

"All kinds of roots": Tim Richardson, *Sweets: A History of Candy* (New York: Bloomsbury, 2002), p. 115.

Tasting Lavender, pages 193 to 197

Renee Shepherd recommends: "Delicious Lavender," *Sunset Magazine* (22 June 2006).

Sweet Parsnips, pages 207 to 211

What'll you have for your supper: "What Did You Have for Your Supper?" is on the Rounder Records album 8001/8002/8003. Sung and played by Peggy and her brother, Mike Seeger, the ninety-four songs on this album are from the book *American Folk Songs for Children*, by their mother, Ruth Crawford Seeger. The book is out of print but still widely available, and the album is available on CD.

Poppies for Seed, pages 213 to 223

In the Czech Republic: A discussion of the alkaloid content of poppy pods is in Vlastimil Miksísk and Václuv Lohr, *The Czech Republic: The Largest Producer of Breadseed Poppy* (Ministry of Agriculture of the Czech Republic, 2020).

The Czechs are probably: Miksísk and Lohr 2020.

Beets for Greens, pages 225 to 231

Jean Bauhin: *Historia Plantarum Universalis*, volume 2 (1651), p. 963.

"Great white Swiss Beet": Thomas Mawe, *The Universal Gardener and Botanist* (London: G. Robinson, 1778).

Cardoon, the artichoke: Botanists disagree about whether the artichoke and the cardoon are the same species. The cardoon is *Cynara cardunculus*; the artichoke is usually called *C. cardunculus* var. *scolymus*. But some botanists prefer to call the artichoke *C. scolymus*. Other French names for chard are *bette à tondre, bette à côte, côtes de bettes, poirée, poirées a carde, jotte, joute, lotte,* and *hutte*. Beetroot, in French, is *betterave*.

Besides eating them raw: According to William Woys Weaver, many cooks use the stems and throw away the greens, in part, he says, because the leaves turn black after cooking. But both the practice of throwing away the greens and Weaver's reason for it are beyond my experience. *Heirloom Vegetable Gardening* (New York: Henry Holt, 1997), p. 90.

In parts of France: The Gardeners and Farmers of Terre Vivante, *Preserving Food without Freezing or Canning* (White River Junction, Vermont: Chelsea Green, 1999).

'Bright Lights': Be aware that the different colors of this cultivar are on different plants, so you must grow at least several chard plants for an assortment of colors in the garden.

Forgotten but Flavorful Quince, pages 233 to 237

Luther Burbank: *How Plants Are Trained to Work for Man, vol III: Fruit Improvement* (New York: P. F. Collier & Son, 1914), p. 246.

Oca, the Tart Little Tuber, pages 239 to 243

My oca crop: Find Bill Whitson's detailed advice on growing oca in "Oca (Oxalis tuberosa)," cultivariable.com/instructions/andean-roots-tubers/how-to-grow-oca/. You can order tubers for planting from Whitson's website, Cultivariable, as well as from Nichols, Raintree, or Annie's Annuals.

William Woys Weaver has a trick: "How to Grow Oca," *Mother Earth News* (1 August 2007).

Jerusalem Fartichokes, pages 245 to 255

The Jerusalem part: The discussion of the early naming of this plant is from C. C. Lacaita, "The 'Jerusalem Artichoke' (*Helianthus tuberosus*)," *Royal Botanic Gardens Bulletin of Miscellaneous Information* 9: pp. 321–39 (1919). Because Sir Philip Sidney, in his poem "Arcadia," used the word *Gyrosol* poetically in 1586, I conclude that the term was somewhat familiar in England in the early seventeenth century, although in 1586 it referred not to *Helianthus* but to the heliotrope.

Louis Eustache Ude: Ude's "potage à la Palestine," was introduced on p. 481 of the 14th edition of his book, *The French Cook* (London: Ebers and Co., 1841).

"Le goust d'artichaut": H. P. Biggar, *The Works of Samuel de Champlain*, vol. 1 (Toronto: Champlain Society, 1922), p. 851.

"Filthy loathsome stinking winde": John Goodyer is quoted in John Gerard's *Herball* (1621), p. 754. Goodyer exaggerated. The "wind" is not filthy or stinking, just noisy and somewhat painful.

Harold McGee. *The Curious Cook* (New York: Macmillan, 1990), p. 84.

"Breedeth melancholy": Tobias Venner, *Via Recta ad Vitam Longam* (London: Henry Hood, 1620), p. 182.

Inulin is highly soluble: McGee 1990, p. 79.

Several scientific studies: Xia Zhang, et al., "Extraction and Purification of Inulin from Jerusalem Artichoke with Response Surface Method and Ion Exchange Resins," *ACS Omega* 7, no. 14 (2022): pp. 12,048–55; Wei Lingyun, et al., "Studies on the Extracting Technical Conditions of Inulin from Jerusalem Tubers," *Journal of Food Engineering* 79, no. 3 (2007): pp. 1,087–93; and Bang-orn Srinameb, et al., "Preparation of Inulin Powder from Jerusalem Artichoke (*Helianthus tuberosus* L.) Tuber," *Plant Foods and Human Nutrition* 70, no. 2 (2015): pp. 221–26.

Fermenting your Jerusalem artichokes: Li Zhang, et al., "Inactivation of Inulinase and Marination of High-Quality Jerusalem Artichoke (*Helianthus tuberosus* L.) Pickles With Screened Dominant Strains," *Frontiers in Bioengineering and Biotechnology* (20 January 2021). Unlike me, these researchers aimed to preserve the inulin in fermented Jerusalem artichokes—because it's good for you! They used ultrasound to do it.

FURTHER READING

David, Edward H., and John T. Morgan. *Collards: A Southern Tradition from Seed to Table*. Tuscaloosa: University of Alabama Press, 2015.

Deppe, Carol. *The Resilient Gardener: Food Production and Self-Reliance in Uncertain Times*. White River Junction, Vermont: Chelsea Green, 2010.

Fussell, Betty. *I Hear America Cooking*. New York: Viking, 1986.

Gibbons, Euell. *Stalking the Wild Asparagus*. New York: David McKay, 1962.

Gin, Margaret, and Alfred E. Castle. *Regional Cooking of China*. San Francisco: 101 Productions, 1975.

Gray, Patience. *Honey from a Weed*. New York: Harper & Row, 1986.

Kuo, Irene. *The Key to Chinese Cooking*. New York: Knopf, 1977.

Larkcom, Joy. *Oriental Vegetables: The Complete Guide for Garden and Kitchen*. Tokyo: Kodansha International, 1991.

Lewis, Daphne, and Carol Miles. *Farming Bamboo*. Raleigh, North Carolina: Lulu Press, 2007.

McGee, Harold. *The Curious Cook*. New York: Macmillan, 1990.

Schneider, Elizabeth. *Uncommon Fruits and Vegetables: A Commonsense Guide*. New York: Harper & Row, 1986.

Van Waerebeek, Ruth. *Everybody Eats Well in Belgium Cookbook*. New York: Workman, 1996.

William Woys Weaver. *Heirloom Vegetable Gardening*. New York: Henry Holt and Company, 1997.

Ziedrich, Linda. *The Joy of Jams, Jellies, and Other Sweet Preserves*. Boston: Harvard Common Press, 2009.

———. *The Joy of Pickling*, 3rd ed. Beverly, Massachusetts: Quarto, 2015.

SEED AND PLANT SUPPLIERS

The foods named in parentheses are those discussed in this book for which the vendor is an excellent source. Most of these vendors sell many other products. I encourage you to peruse the online catalogs.

Adaptive Seeds (poppies, tomatoes). 25079 Brush Creek Road, Sweet Home, Oregon, 97386. (541) 367-1105. adaptiveseeds.com.

Annie's Annuals (oca). 740 Market Avenue, Richmond, California, 94801. (888) 266-4370. anniesannuals.com.

Artisan Seeds (Fred Hempel's tomatoes). P.O. Box 428, Sunol, California, 94586. (510) 384-2716. growartisan.com.

Baker Creek Heirloom Seeds (tomatoes). 2778 Baker Creek Road, Mansfield, Missouri, 65704. rareseeds.com.

Cultivariable (potatoes, oca). P.O. Box 111, Moclips, Washington, 98562. cultivariable.com.

Egyptian Walking Onion. (509) 554-3842. egyptian-walkingonion.com.

Hazzard's Seeds (violets). P.O. Box 151, Deford, Michigan, 48729. (989) 872-5057. hazzardsgreenhouse.com.

Irish Eyes Garden Seeds (potatoes). 5045 Robinson Canyon Road, Ellensburg, Washington, 98926. (509) 933-7150. irisheyesgardenseeds.com.

Johnny's Selected Seeds (shiso). 955 Benton Avenue, Winslow, Maine, 04901. (877) 564-6697. johnnyseeds.com.

Kitazawa Seed Company (garlic chives, shiso). 175 West 2700 South, Salt Lake City, Utah, 84115. (510) 595-1188. kitazawaseed.com.

Nichols Garden Nursery (lavender, oca, tomatoes). 1136 Main Street, Philomath, Oregon, 97370. (800) 422-3985. nicholsgardennursery.com.

One Green World (quinces, honeyberries). 6469 Southeast 134th Avenue, Portland, Oregon, 97236. (877) 353-4028. onegreenworld.com.

Portland Seedhouse (potatoes). portlandseedhouse.com.

Raintree Nursery (oca). 408 Butts Road, Morton, Washington, 98356. (800) 391-8892. raintreenursery.com.

Renee's Garden Seeds (lavender). 6060 Graham Hill Road, Felton, California, 95018. (888) 880-7228. reneesgarden.com.

Seed Savers Exchange (tomatoes, garbanzos, citron melon, Jerusalem artichoke). 3094 North Winn Road, Decorah, Iowa, 52101. (563) 382-5990. seedsavers.org.

Select Seeds (violets). 180 Stickney Hill Road, Union, Connecticut, 06076. (800) 684-0395. selectseeds.com.

Southern Exposure Seed Exchange (collards). P.O. Box 460, Mineral, Virginia, 23117. (540) 894-9480. southernexposure.com.

Swallowtail Garden Seeds (violets). 122 Calistoga Road, #178, Santa Rosa, California, 95409. (877) 489-7333. swallowtailgardenseeds.com.

Tomato Growers (tomatoes). P.O. Box 60015, Fort Myers, Florida, 33906. (239) 768-1119. tomatogrowers.com.

Wild Garden Seeds (orach). P.O. Box 1509, Philomath, Oregon, 97370. (541) 929-4068. wildgardenseed.com.

INDEX

Linda Ziedrich writes about food from garden to table, food in history, and food across cultures. At her home in Oregon's Willamette Valley, she continually experiments with the fruits and vegetables that she grows. She is also the author of *First Fruits: The Lewellings and the Birth of the Pacific Coast Fruit Industry*; *The Joy of Pickling*, now in its third edition; and *The Joy of Jams, Jellies, and Other Sweet Preserves*. See her website at agardenerstable.com.